C000001870

Praise for **25 need-to-know s**

"This is a highly practical, punchy and brilliantly written guide to strategy development. It is perfect for managers of large and small businesses who need to make big decisions, but have limited time for long tomes on business theory. An excellent read."

Charles Ind, Managing Partner, Bowmark Capital LLP

"I wish I had written this book: extremely practical and clear, but full of rich content. It is a terrific compendium of all the major strategy tools, brought to life with great examples. Definitely the best strategy book around for people who think they can't read strategy books."

Marcus Alexander, Strategy Professor, London Business School

"This book does a superb job demystifying strategy and bringing it within the reach of anyone who takes the time to read it and apply the tools. Strategy made simple."

Jeff van der Eems, Chief Executive Officer, United Biscuits International

"An excellent guide to setting strategy for businesses large and small. I particularly liked the focus on really understanding the sources of sustainable competitive advantage in the key areas of a business. The techniques described for achieving this, combined with the recommended emphasis on detailed quantitative analysis, will be of great benefit to any enterprise."

Adrian Beecroft, Chairman, Dawn Capital and former Chief Investment Officer, Apax Partners

"A compulsory read for every leader, wherever they sit in a firm. These are 25 need-to-know tools to help them devise robust plans to get the business from A to B and help win the commitment of their teams."

Ian Armitage, former Managing Partner, HgCapital

"Of all the books on business strategy, this is the most concise, lucid and elegantly structured statement of the current state of knowledge. Brilliant, and beautifully written."

Jules Goddard, Fellow, London Business School

"Here are the main strategy tools, elegantly and vividly described, with the bonus of an often intriguing real life example placed alongside each one, from Samuel Adams to Zara, Marvel to Madonna. Perfect reading for the long distance journey."

Stephen Lawrence, Chief Executive, Protocol Education Ltd and former Managing Director, Arthur D. Little

"A concise distillation of the writer's deep knowledge of strategic thinking, distilled into a highly readable format. Even the busiest executive should find time to read these excellent 25 pointers."

Vince O'Brien, Director, Montagu Private Equity LLP

"Like economists, no two business strategists will come up with the same list of 25 most important strategy tools. But Evans makes his case well and sets out his selection lucidly. And the ratio of one case study per tool adds both relevance and zip to the book. A terrific read."

Christine Harvey, former Director of Business Analysis and Planning, GlaxoSmithKline R&D

"This book offers a refreshing insight into the core strategy tools. Compelling reading for all."

Mike Garland, Head of Portfolio Group, Permira Advisers LLP

"An excellent book. I like the simple approach of just a short description plus a terrific case study per tool. This is the sort of book you can use in a number of ways depending on your familiarity with strategy and your time available. It can either be a great read when flying to that business meeting or you can pick it up, read a section and put it down again without losing the thread. The author acknowledges that strategy is 90 per cent common sense, but you need a framework and a set of tools to corral those ideas into a credible business strategy. This book does that, and more. It is a 'must have' for any manager making the leap from a series of great ideas to structuring a strategy, and an easy to use reference volume for the more experienced individual. The book doesn't have everything, it isn't meant to, but what it contains is excellent, and very readable – ideal for a busy manager in a time poor modern business world."

Grahame Hughes, Founding Director, Haven Power Ltd

"Evans' earlier book on key strategy tools was a most useful reference, but there were an awful lot of them. The 25 here are easier to handle – and this time there's a stimulating example to illustrate each one. This book is as readable as you'll find in the genre."

Jonathan Derry-Evans, Partner, Manfield Partners

25 need-to-know strategy tools

PEARSON

At Pearson, we believe in learning – all kinds of learning for all kinds of people. Whether it's at home, in the classroom or in the workplace, learning is the key to improving our life chances.

That's why we're working with leading authors to bring you the latest thinking and best practices, so you can get better at the things that are important to you. You can learn on the page or on the move, and with content that's always crafted to help you understand quickly and apply what you've learned.

If you want to upgrade your personal skills or accelerate your career, become a more effective leader or more powerful communicator, discover new opportunities or simply find more inspiration, we can help you make progress in your work and life.

Pearson is the world's leading learning company. Our portfolio includes the Financial Times and our education business, Pearson International.

Every day our work helps learning flourish, and wherever learning flourishes, so do people.

To learn more, please visit us at **www.pearson.com/uk**

The Financial Times

With a worldwide network of highly respected journalists, *The Financial Times* provides global business news, insightful opinion and expert analysis of business, finance and politics. With over 500 journalists reporting from 50 countries worldwide, our in-depth coverage of international news is objectively reported and analysed from an independent, global perspective.

To find out more, visit **www.ft.com/pearsonoffer/**

25 need-to-know strategy tools

Vaughan Evans

PEARSON

Harlow, England • London • New York • Boston • San Francisco • Toronto • Sydney
Auckland • Singapore • Hong Kong • Tokyo • Seoul • Taipei • New Delhi
Cape Town • São Paulo • Mexico City • Madrid • Amsterdam • Munich • Paris • Milan

Pearson Education Limited
Edinburgh Gate
Harlow CM20 2JE
United Kingdom
Tel: +44 (0)1279 623623
Web: www.pearson.com/uk

First published 2014 (print and electronic)

© VEP (UK) Limited 2014 (print and electronic)

Pearson Education is not responsible for the content of third-party internet sites.

ISBN: 978–1–292–01643–6 (print)
978–1–292–01645–0 (PDF)
978–1–292–01646–7 (ePub)
978–1–292–01644–3 (eText)

British Library Cataloguing-in-Publication Data
A catalogue record for the print edition is available from the British Library

Library of Congress Cataloging-in-Publication Data
Evans, Vaughan, 1951-
  25 need-to-know strategy tools / Vaughan Evans.
    pages cm
  Includes bibliographical references and index.
  ISBN 978-1-292-01643-6 (print) -- ISBN 978-1-292-01645-0 (PDF) -- ISBN 978-1-292-
01646-7 (ePub) -- ISBN 978-1-292-01644-3 (eText)
  1. Strategic planning. 2. Organizational effectiveness. 3. Management. I. Title. II.
Title: Twenty-five need-to-know strategy tools.
  HD30.28.E932 2014
  658.4'012--dc23
                        2014028348

The print publication is protected by copyright. Prior to any prohibited
reproduction, storage in a retrieval system, distribution or transmission in any form
or by any means, electronic, mechanical, recording or otherwise, permission should
be obtained from the publisher or, where applicable, a licence permitting restricted
copying in the United Kingdom should be obtained from the Copyright Licensing
Agency Ltd, Saffron House, 6–10 Kirby Street, London EC1N 8TS.

The ePublication is protected by copyright and must not be copied, reproduced,
transferred, distributed, leased, licensed or publicly performed or used in any way
except as specifically permitted in writing by the publishers, as allowed under the
terms and conditions under which it was purchased, or as strictly permitted by
applicable copyright law. Any unauthorised distribution or use of this text may be a
direct infringement of the author's and the publishers' rights and those responsible
may be liable in law accordingly.

All trademarks used herein are the property of their respective owners. The use of
any trademark in this text does not vest in the author or publisher any trademark
ownership rights in such trademarks, nor does the use of such trademarks imply any
affiliation with or endorsement of this book by such owners.

10 9 8 7 6 5 4 3 2
18 17 16 15

Cover design: Two Associates
Print edition typeset in 9pt StoneSerif by30
Print edition printed and bound in Great Britain by Henry Ling Ltd., at the Dorset
Press, Dorchester, Dorset

NOTE THAT ANY PAGE CROSS REFERENCES REFER TO THE PRINT EDITION

To Carys, Tool 25...!

Contents

About the author

Vaughan Evans is an independent strategy consultant (**www. vaughanevansandpartners.com**) specialising in strategy and business planning for corporate clients and strategic due diligence for private equity.

An economics graduate from Cambridge University and an Alfred P. Sloan fellow with distinction from London Business School, Vaughan worked for many years at international management and technology consultants Arthur D. Little and at investment bankers Bankers Trust Co.

Vaughan is also a popular speaker and seminar leader, and regularly delivers speeches on how to keep strategy simple yet backable.

He is the author of a number of successful business books, including *The Financial Times Essential Guide to Developing a Business Strategy* (2013), the highly acclaimed *Key Strategy Tools* (2012) and the best-selling *The Financial Times Essential Guide to Writing a Business Plan: How to Win Backing to Start Up or Grow Your Business* (2011).

Publisher's acknowledgements

We are grateful to the following for permission to reproduce copyright material:

Figures

Figure 4.1 from *Building Your Company's Vision* by Jim Collins and Jerry Porras. Copyright © 1996. Reprinted with permission of Curtis Brown, Ltd.; Figure 6.1 adapted with the permission of Simon & Schuster Publishing Group from the Free Press edition of COMPETITIVE STRATEGY: Techniques for Analyzing Industries and Competitors by Michael E. Porter. Copyright © 1980 1998 by The Free Press. All rights reserved; Figure 8.1 from *Contemporary Strategy Analysis*, Grant, Robert M. Copyright © Robert M. Grant. Reproduced with permission of John Wiley & Sons Inc.; Figure 9.1 adapted with the permission of Simon & Schuster Publishing Group from the Free Press edition of COMPETITIVE STRATEGY: Creating and Sustaining Superior Performance by Michael E. Porter. Copyright © 1985 1998 by Michael E. Porter. All rights reserved; Figure 10.1 adapted from Strategies for Diversification, *Harvard Business Review*, Sept-Oct, pp.1113-25 (Ansoff, I. 1957); Figure 12.1 adapted from The BCG Portfolio Matrix from the Product Portfolio Matrix, © 1970, The Boston Consulting Group; Figure 15.1 adapted from *Blue Ocean Strategy: How to Create Uncontested Market Space and Make the Competition Irrelevant*, Harvard Business School Press (Chan Kim, W. and Mauborgne, R. 2005) p.98, Figure 4.6; Figure 15.2 adapted from *Blue Ocean Strategy: How to Create Uncontested Market Space and Make the Competition Irrelevant*, Harvard Business School Press (Chan Kim, W. and Mauborgne, R. 2005) p.29 Figure 2.2; Figures 16.1 and 16.3 adapted from The

BCG Portfolio Matrix from the Product Portfolio Matrix, © 1970, The Boston Consulting Group; Figure 18.1 from *Corporate-Level Strategy: Creating Value in Multi-Business Companies* John Wiley & Sons (Goold, M. Campbell, A. and Alexander, M. 1994) Figure 2.3; Figure 19.1 adapted from *Competing for the Future*, Harvard Business School Press (Hamel, G. and Prahalad, C.K. 1994); Figure 20.1 adapted from *The Rise and Fall of Strategic Planning* by Mintzberg, H., Pearson Education Limited © 2000 Pearson Education Limited and adapted with the permission of Simon & Schuster Publishing Group from the Free Press edition of THE RISE AND FALL OF STRATEGIC PLANNING by Henry Mintzberg. Copyright © 1994 by Henry Mintzberg. All rights reserved; Figure 21.1 from *Unstoppable: finding hidden assets to renew the core and fuel profitable growth*, Harvard Business School Publishing (Zook, C. 2007) p.29, Figure 2-1; Figure 21.2 adapted from *Profit from the Core*, Harvard Business School Press (Zook, C. 2001) p.74, Figure 3-1; Figure 22.1 adapted from *The Innovator's Dilemma*, Harvard Business School Press (Christensen, C. M. 1997); Figure 24.1 reprinted with permission of the publisher. From *Hot Spots*, copyright © 2007 by Gratton, L., Berrett-Koehler Publishers, Inc., San Francisco, CA.

Tables

Table 19.1 adapted from *Competing for the Future*, Harvard Business School Press (Hamel, G. and Prahalad, C.K. 1994) p.26.

In some instances we have been unable to trace the owners of copyright material, and we would appreciate any information that would enable us to do so.

Introduction

Your clue is in the title: need-to-know . . .

This book's aim is simple. It presents a set of tools that you, as a manager or entrepreneur, need to know. These are the basic tools of strategy, the essentials you need to do your job effectively.

This is not a complete strategy toolkit. Nor is it a do-it-yourself manual. And it certainly isn't a strategy textbook for the business school student. Other excellent books serve all these purposes.

Nor is this, necessarily, a book on the latest, cutting-edge thinking in strategy. There is some of that, but only where such tools have already become essential.

This is a book on what you **need to know** about the tools of strategy. No more, no less.

It is restricted to 25 tools because these are the core elements you need on a day-to-day basis in your strategic planning. It is designed for busy business people who want a curated set of tools that will help them achieve the best results in the shortest amount of time.

If, after reading this book, you want to dig deeper into the full set of strategy tools, these are contained in a companion book, *Key Strategy Tools: The 80+ Tools for Every Manager to Build a Winning Strategy* (Pearson, 2012).

What is 'strategy'?

'Strategy' has a myriad of definitions. General Sun Tzu in the 6th century BC defined it as 'know your opponent', while rather more recently Kenichi Ohmae summed it up as 'in a word, competitive advantage' (that's actually two words, but who's counting?!).

I am an economist by training, so feel the need to bring the word 'resources' into a broader definition. Economics is succinctly defined as the optimal allocation of a nation's scarce resources. Thus, at the micro-economic level: 'Strategy is how a firm achieves its goals by deploying its scarce resources to gain a sustainable competitive advantage'.

The tools here are not arranged randomly, nor are they listed in some meaningless order such as by the originator's alphabetical name.

They are presented in the order in which they would be deployed typically in a strategy development process.

One such process introduced in this book's more voluminous companion, *Key Strategy Tools* (referred to above), is the Strategy Pyramid. This consists of nine building blocks (see Figure 0.1).

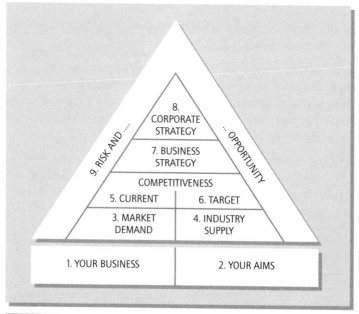

Figure 0.1 **The nine building blocks of the Strategy Pyramid**

The tools of this book are set out following the same process:

Block 1 Knowing your business – see Tool 1 of this book

Block 2 Setting goals and objectives – see Tools 2–4 (including Collins and Porras's big, hairy, audacious goals)

Block 3 Forecasting market demand – see Tool 5

Block 4 Gauging industry competition – see Tool 6 (Porter's five forces, of course!)

Block 5 Tracking competitive advantage – see Tools 7–10

Block 6 Targeting the strategic gap – see Tools 11–12

Block 7 Bridging the gap with business strategy – see Tools 13–15 (including Kim and Mauborgne's blue ocean strategy)

Block 8 Bridging the gap with corporate strategy – see Tools 16–24 (including tools from Hamel and Prahalad, Mintzberg, Christensen and Rumelt)

Block 9 Addressing risk and opportunity – see Tool 25.

You can read *25 Need-to-Know Strategy Tools* either from beginning to end, following a logical strategy development process, or you can just dip in and out, when you want – as you please.

But remember that this book doesn't cover everything there is to know about strategy – if you need to know more, some further reading is suggested at the end of the book.

Do not be dismayed by strategy or strategic thinking. I often meet business folk who preface their strategic insights by saying: 'Unfortunately I have never had any training in strategy, but what I think is...'

Such humility is endearing but misplaced. Strategy is 90 per cent common sense. That many managers and entrepreneurs treat it with such awe is partly down to my own profession of strategy consulting. It is, I am afraid, in the commercial interests of many of my peers to maintain the myth.

Not so in this book. You will find that it is written in an easy-to-read style. Jargon is avoided wherever possible. And tools are related to the real world.

I have chosen tools that will help you in your business. These are not tools that are just clever, designed to give one smart professor at one prominent business school bragging rights over another. These are tools that can be used – by you.

Pocket the huge sums that you would otherwise pay to consultants. Read this book and let it be your guide on how to use strategy tools for the benefit of your business.

To help you on the way, I have added one case study per tool of how one company, typically well known, has used the tool effectively – or, in some cases, should have used it!

Strategy is all about direction. You want to get your business from where it is today to where you want it to be tomorrow.

Let this book help you get there.

Enjoy!

Business vs corporate strategy

One thing we need to address upfront is how this book approaches the two distinct, but related, fields of strategy: business strategy and corporate strategy. A business, or, more technically, a strategic business unit (SBU), is defined as an entity with a closely inter-related product (or service) offering and a cost structure largely independent of other business units. Thus, in a large, multi-business corporation, an SBU may well have not only its own CEO, CFO, COO, CSMO and CIO, but its own CTO, head of all R&D in that SBU.

An SBU is an entity substantive enough to warrant drawing up its own strategy, independent of strategies its fellow SBUs may be drawing up.

SBU strategy is known more simply as business strategy. Tools 1–15 of this book deal with business strategy.

Corporate strategy is, in the first instance, how you allocate resources between your businesses. Which will you invest in, which will you hold for cash generation, which will you sell, which may you be forced to close down? This is corporate strategy as portfolio planning – see Tool 16, Optimising the corporate portfolio.

But corporate strategy is more than that. It is about how you strive to attain synergies between your businesses, how you create value in the centre, how you initiate a winning culture or capability that permeates the entire organisation. This is the resource-based theory of corporate strategy – see, for example, Tool 19, Hamel and Prahalad's core competences.

Business and corporate strategy can be a movable feast. A multi-business company may hive off a business unit as a separate entity, which may then set up its own SBUs. What was business strategy, as part of a parent's corporate strategy, one day becomes the corporate strategy of an independent company the next.

Top 10 do's and don'ts of strategy development

Top 5 do's

1. Do: follow a structured process

Start at step one and work through to the last, lest you leave out a key step. One such process is the Strategy Pyramid, set out in the introduction to this book. A recent client of mine built in no competitive response to his modelling of strategic options, partly because he had relegated analysis of competition to a single paragraph earlier in the document. Each step in the strategy development process has a purpose.

2. Do: define your vision

Don't dive head first into markets and competitive positioning. Set out your vision or goals first. Another client asked for help with evaluating strategic options, which was nigh on impossible because her senior management team had never done step one, clarifying the organisation's vision. Vision should drive strategy and inspire implementation – through the use, perhaps, of big, hairy, audacious goals (Tool 4).

3. Do: understand the market

Analyse aggregate demand, customer behaviour and your competitive environment every which way. Shove it all into an appendix, or even into a virtual appendix to the printed appendix, and pull out the main drivers for your strategy document. You never know when you might have recourse to snippets of that market analysis. No subsequent analysis of your competitive position, your strategic gap or your alternatives for bridging that gap will have any validity unless underpinned by the solid foundation of market understanding.

4. Do: convert bubbles into numbers

Bubbles are the darlings of strategists, even more so of strategy consultants. No section is complete without a 2 × 2 matrix with bubbles floating around. I should know – I love composing these works of bubble art. But they are necessary, not sufficient, tools for strategy development. They need to be backed up by hard numbers and simple modelling. Conclusions based on favourable bubble positioning can often peter away to insignificance once modelled. Strategic options featuring price adjustments are frequent culprits – an option suggesting a price discount for a related product upon purchase of another product may sound strategically wise, but model the impact on revenues of the **possible** volume increase along with the **given** price reduction and the option may no longer seem so smart.

5. Do: remember risk

It is curious how so many strategy documents fail to conclude with an assessment of risk and opportunity. This never happens in strategic due diligence, undertaken when a company or finance house is poised to invest in or buy out a target, so why should it happen in strategy, the purpose of which is to allocate investment resources in a particular direction? The same tools could and should be used in strategy development (see the Suns & Clouds Chart, Tool 25).

Top 5 don'ts

1. Don't: use tools indiscriminately

Just because a tool is in this book – or in its older and weightier sister, *Key Strategy Tools*, which features 88 of them – doesn't mean that you have to use it. Use it only if you assess it as being relevant to your company in your situation in your industry. Of course, some tools should always be used. No strategy development exercise would be complete without, for example, the Five Forces (Tool 6), the attractiveness/advantage matrix (Tool 11) or, I would argue, the Suns & Clouds Chart (Tool 25). But pick and choose others with care.

2. Don't: underestimate the competition

It does wonders for organisational morale to have a dig at the competition now and again. But what is good for the chat round the water cooler is not good at all for the strategy workshop. Who are they? What are they up to? What could they be up to? In your worst nightmare, what could they do to you? It is as well to be prepared. Build such thoughts into your risk analysis and mitigate accordingly.

3. Don't: forget competitive response

This is related to the previous don't, but is different and the distinction is important. This book relates to developing your organisation's strategy. Once this is done and the strategy is put into effect, what then? Will the competition lie on its back and ask you to tickle its tummy? No. If your strategy is worth its weight, your competitors will respond. They will have to. Be prepared and build that response into your modelling of strategic options.

4. Don't: write a thesis

Recently I came across a strategy document that ran to over 200 pages of well-written, well-analysed text. But I couldn't, for the devil of me, find a strategy. A strategy document has to be digestible to your board directors, including non-executives, who will be less well versed in the intricacies of your organisation and, potentially, to outside investors. It must be clear, concise and non-esoteric. All relevant detail should be arranged in appendices. It should be punchy – which is why I favour the use of PowerPoint, which forces you to write a conclusion for each slide, rather than Word. And, ultimately, it should be conclusive: the title of the executive summary slide should encapsulate the derived strategy in one sentence.

5. Don't: bow to ego

Most acquisitions fail – see Tool 17 – and one of the main reasons for that is empire building by the CEO and perhaps the whole senior management team. So, too, many organic strategies will fail when they rest on the ego or self-enrichment desires of management. Base your strategy on an understanding of the market environment, the creation of a sustainable competitive advantage and an assessment of risk and opportunity – not on ego.

Identifying key segments

This tool will help you:

- Discover where value resides in your business
- Focus your strategy on the segments that count
- Allocate your resources most effectively

About this tool

How well do you know your business? In which deep, dark recesses do – or will – the profits reside?

Does your firm serve some segments where you generate good sales but frustratingly little profit? And what of those merrier segments where sales are modest but margins meaty?

There are two components to identifying key business segments:

- Which segments does your firm compete in – which products (or services) do you – or will you – sell to which sets of customers?
- Which of these segments delivers the most profit?

Only once this segmentation process is complete should you embark on developing your strategy. There is no point devoting hours of research, whether in analysing competitor data or gathering customer feedback, in a segment that contributes to just 1 per cent of your operating profit – and that offers little prospect of growing that contribution over the next five years.

How you could strengthen your capabilities in that segment may be fascinating, but is not material to your business strategy and is of little interest to your board or backer.

You need to devote your time and effort to strengthening your firm's presence in those segments that contribute, or will contribute, to 80 per cent or more of your business.

How to use it

In an established business

What is your business mix? What products or services does your business offer and to which customer groups?

Which count for most in your business?

Businesses seldom offer just the one product to one customer group. Most businesses offer a number of distinct products to a number of distinct customer groups.

A product tends to be distinctive if the competition differs from one product to another. Some competitors may offer all your services; others may specialise in one or two of them. Others still may offer just the one as a spin-off to a largely unrelated business.

A customer group is distinctive if the customers have distinct characteristics and are reachable typically through distinct marketing routes.

Thus a customer group can be defined by who they are (e.g. leisure or business visitor, young or old, well or less educated), what sector they are in (especially for business-to-business ventures), where they are located (e.g. town or suburbs, region, country) or in other ways where different marketing approaches will be needed to reach them.

Each distinct product offered to a distinct customer group is a segment, termed, in rather ungainly business-speak, a 'product/ market segment' or, more simply, a 'business segment'.

If your business offers two products to one customer group, you have two business segments. If you stick with the same two products but develop a new customer group, you'll have four segments. Introduce a third product and sell it to both customer groups and you have six segments.

How many products does your business offer? To how many customer groups? Multiply the two numbers together and that's how many business segments you serve.

Now, which two, three or four segments are the most important? Which contribute most to sales? We assume at this stage that each segment has a similar cost profile, so the proportionate contribution of each to sales is the same as that to operating profit.

And what of the future? Will these same segments be the main contributors to sales over the next few years?

Set this out precisely and succinctly here. In too many strategic plans this basic information is absent. Often one sees a pie chart or two of sales by main product line, or sales by region or country. This is useful, but it could be much more so. What is left out is:

▨ Sales by product/market segment – that is, sales of a specific product line **to a specific customer group**

▨ That same information over time, say over the last three years.

Let's take a simple example. Your company makes widgets, small, medium and large, which you sell to three sectors, manufacturing, engineering and construction, in each of two countries, UK and France. You operate in 3 * 3 * 2 = 18 product/market segments.

By far your biggest segment is large widgets to UK engineering, which account for 40 per cent of sales. This is followed by medium widgets to UK engineering at 25 per cent of sales and large widgets to French manufacturing at 15 per cent of sales. Together these three segments account for 80 per cent of sales.

The remaining 15 segments account for just 20 per cent of sales – see Figure 1.1.

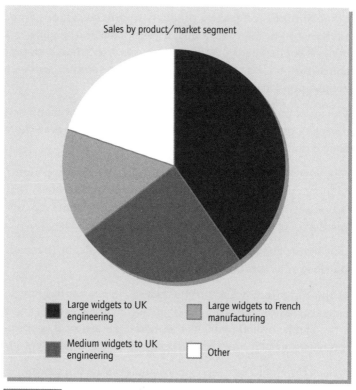

Figure 1.1 Key segmentation: an example

Very often, what would be set out here would be a pie chart showing a breakdown of sales by widget size – large, medium and small. Alongside might be another pie chart showing sales by country – UK and France. Better, it might combine both country and end-user data, breaking down sales into four customer groups – UK engineering, UK manufacturing, French engineering and French manufacturing.

This is useful information, but what would be very much more useful would be a pie chart showing the real product/market

segmentation as set out above. It would show or /
– large widgets to UK engineering – accounting for 4̶
sales and another for 25 per cent.

That would show that the key issues impacting on your firm's
strategy development, whether relating to market demand, competition or your firm's competitiveness, are those pertaining to
one particular segment – large widgets to UK engineering. Not
large widgets in general, not small widgets, not UK as a whole,
not all of France, not French engineering, not UK construction,
but specifically one product/market segment – large widgets to
UK engineering.

Engineering customers will have different demand influences
than those in construction. The UK may be at a different stage
in the economic cycle to France. French engineering companies
may have different solutions favouring medium over large widgets. Small widget producers may be more numerous and have
more flexible, short-run production facilities than those making
large widgets.

For any or all of these reasons, you need to know that one prod-
uct/market segment – large widgets to UK engineering – matters
most in your business. And what matters next is the segment of
medium widgets to UK engineering, followed by large widgets to
French manufacturing.

And what of the future? Perhaps you are set to launch an extra-
large widget tailored to the UK aerospace sector, which, if all goes
to plan, could account for 20 per cent of sales in three years' time.

So let's have a second pie chart alongside the first showing forecast sales by main product/market segment in three years' time.

And what of profitability? So far we have assumed that each segment has the same cost structure. This is unlikely to be so.

We need to repeat the exercise examining each segment's contribution not to sales, but to operating profit.

That data may not exist. Surely you have sales by product/market
segment and probably gross profit, too.

But it is operating profit, or at least contribution to fixed overheads, that we need. Some segments will be heavier consumers of the marketing budget or travel expenses than others.

The data that emerges from your management information system may not give this level of detail. In that case you need to make estimates. Reasoned estimates are far better than no data. After all, soon you will be making reasoned judgement on a whole range of external factors, like market demand and industry competition, in drawing up your strategy.

The contribution of key segments to operating profit will differ from that for sales. Some segments will be more profitable than others. More profitable segments will have a higher share of operating profit than sales.

But that doesn't mean that the breakdown by operating profit is necessarily more useful than that by sales. The latter can highlight where profitability in certain segments is lagging behind others and potentially how that gap can be narrowed.

Returning to the example of the engineering company, where the segment of large widgets to UK engineering contributes to 40 per cent of sales: suppose the contribution to operating profit was only 30 per cent, the same as that of the second largest segment (in terms of sales), medium widgets to UK engineering – despite the latter contributing to only 25 per cent of sales.

Both sets of data are important. There may be structural factors influencing the disparity in profitability – the large widget business may face competition from Far Eastern imports, unlike with medium widgets. This will limit the firm's choice of strategic options.

But it may be that the firm's manufacturing efficiency has fallen behind that of its domestic competitors, which have invested in capital equipment ideally suited for the larger widgets. This will lie within the firm's scope to act.

In a start-up venture

If you are planning a business start-up, you may still neeι. ment. If you are to launch just the one product (or service) to oι. group of customers, fine, you won't need to segment any further. But are you sure you'll have only one product? And only one customer group?

Try categorising your products. And your customers. Is further segmentation meaningful? If so, use it. If not, don't waste time just for the sake of seeming serious. Stick to the one product for the one customer group, i.e. one business segment.

But there is one big difference. No matter how you segment, no matter how many customer groups you identify, they are all, at present, gleams in the eye.

You have no customers. Yet.

Your product must be couched in terms of its benefits to the customer. That is the business proposition.

Not the way in which your product can do this, do that, at this price. But in the way in which your product or service can **benefit** the target customer.

Who is the target customer? In which way will he or she benefit from your offering?

And that is just in the one segment. Are there others?

Segmentation may lie at the very heart of your business proposition. It may have been in the very act of segmentation that you unearthed a niche where only your offering can yield the customer benefit. And you have since tailored your offering to address that very niche, that customer benefit.

For further stimulating thoughts on this, see the chapter on 'Will the fish bite?' in John Mullins' indispensable guide to business start-ups, *The New Business Road Test: What Entrepreneurs and Executives Should Do Before Writing a Business Plan* – and also my investor-focused book, *FT Essential Guide to Writing a Business Plan: How to Win Backing to Start Up or Grow your Business.*

Here is a slightly different way of looking at it. Does your offering address some 'unmet need' in the marketplace? Does it fill a gap in a target customer's needs? This is one of the secrets to a new venture's success highlighted by William Bridges in his book, *Creating You & Co*. He suggests that an 'unmet need' could be uncovered by spotting signs such as a missing piece in a pattern, an unrecognised opportunity, an underused resource, a signal event, an unacknowledged change, a supposedly impossible situation, a non-existent but needed service, a new or emerging problem, a bottleneck, an interface, or other similar signs.

However you define the customer benefit, whether in terms of unmet needs or in a way more meaningful to your offering, you need to undertake some basic research to dig up whatever evidence you can glean of customer benefit.

An understanding of customer benefit will help you to clarify segmentation.

In summary, this essential tool highlights what matters most in your business mix, now and in the near future. Which product/ market segments will make or break your business?

When to use it – or be wary

You should use segmentation at the very start of the strategy development process, always. It is critical.

Be careful, though, of paralysis through analysis. Don't end up with dozens of segments. Concentrate on the half-dozen or so product/ market segments that truly drive your firm's value creation.

Using it: IBM

IBM bestrode the global computer industry in the 1980s. It was virtually a generic name for mainframes, mini-computers and, later, personal computers, like Hoover in vacuum cleaning.

Then, in the early 1990s, the world caught up with Big Blue. Growth slowed, profits tumbled. Lou Gerstner, marketer not technologist, was brought in to turn things round. 'What happened to this company was not an act of God, some mysterious biblical plague sent down from on high,' he told his managers. 'It's simple. People took our business away.'

IBM had become too siloed, too inward looking, too distant from customer needs. Gerstner transformed the culture – and the strategic direction. In 1990 IBM was, essentially, a hardware manufacturer, from where came two-thirds of revenues, with the remaining one-third split between software and services.

Ten years later services and software accounted for three-fifths. Further rationalisation followed – the personal computer business, along with the Think Pad laptop, was sold to the Chinese producer, Lenovo. Today, services alone account for 55 per cent of a $60 billion turnover.

Companies evolve. Business unit profitability changes over time, likewise segments within business units, so good managers redeploy resources accordingly. A small segment today could be a big business tomorrow – think of Nokia and its cell phones, Apple and its iPad. Or IBM and its Global Services division.

Know your business. Identify the key segments.

2

Setting long-term goals

This tool will help you:

- Gain guidance on strategic direction and values
- Provide a framework for assessing strategic alternatives
- Avoid risks of strategic deviation

About this tool

D'où venons nous? Que sommes nous? Où allons nous? (Where do we come from? What are we? Where are we going?) inscribed Paul Gauguin on his hauntingly existential Tahitian painting, in those long distant post-Impressionist days when art was artistic. You dealt with the first two questions in the first tool, now for the third: where are you going?

Goal setting is the cornerstone of business strategy. Goals should underpin each of your company's main strategic initiatives over the next five years or so.

There are numerous treatises on the relative merits of a company articulating its vision, mission, aims, purposes, goals, objectives, values, principles, ideals, beliefs and so on. The sound of hair splitting can be deafening.

It is simpler and adequate to stick to two of these: goals and objectives.

A goal is something your business aims to be, as described in words. An objective is a target that helps to measure whether that goal is achieved, and typically is set out in numbers.

One of your goals may be for your business to be the most customer-centric supplier of your services in Northern Europe. Objectives to back up that goal could be the achievement of a 'highly satisfied' rating of 30 per cent from your annual customer survey by 2014 and 35 per cent by 2016, along with 80 per cent 'satisfied' or better by that year.

Goals are directional, objectives are specific. The former should look beyond the short term and set out where you see the firm in the long term. The latter should be SMART, namely Specific, Measurable, Attainable, Relevant and Time-limited – see the next tool.

Other aims can readily slot into the simple goals and objectives framework:

- Mission – in theory, what sets your business apart from the rest of the competition; in practice, you can treat this as a goal
- Vision – in theory, where your business aims to go or become; again, you can treat this as another goal
- Aims – they can be taken as roughly synonymous with goals
- Purposes – ditto
- Values – in theory, a set of beliefs and principles that guide how your business should respond when there are moral, ethical, safety, health, environmental or other value-related demands on the business that may conflict with the goal of shareholder value maximisation; in practice, these can be identified as separate goals
- Beliefs – as for values
- Ideals – ditto
- Principles – ditto.

Goal setting should also prove motivational. Goals can enhance employee performance in four ways, according to Latham and Locke:

1   They focus attention towards goal-relevant activities
2   They have an energising effect
3   They encourage persistence
4   They help staff cope with the task to hand.

The setting of long-term goals and SMART objectives is an essential tool in strategy development.

How to use it

Here are five considerations when setting goals:

1   Goals differ from objectives
2   Short-term goals have little place in strategy development
3   The best goals for motivational purposes may be market-related
4   Financial goals may need to resolve the shareholder-stakeholder trade-off
5   Value-related goals are no less valid.

Firstly, a goal is something your business aims to be, as described in words. An objective is a target that helps to measure whether that goal is achieved, and typically is set out in numbers. Your goal may be to become a low-cost provider in a key segment. An accompanying objective might be to reduce unit operating costs in that segment within three years by 10 per cent.

Second, think of short-term goals as what lies within and behind this year's budget. These may be important in the short term, whether for keeping the financial markets or your private owners happy or for you landing that performance-related bonus.

But what lies within that budget may have little impact on strategy development. Strategy takes into account market demand trends and industry competition forces that go well beyond the short term. It is no good gearing up your business to compete ferociously in the short term only to be exposed to a drop-off in demand or intensified competition in the medium to long term.

Third, there are various types of goal. Market- or customer-oriented goals are often the most motivational and are easy enough to monitor. Market share data is collected readily by companies beyond a certain size. A goal could be market leadership in segment A within three years. Such a goal is motivational for the salesforce, and it is often simple to assess progress.

Customer satisfaction or retention goals (or objectives – see the next tool) can also have the same effect.

Operational goals are also incentivising for the operations team – and even simpler to monitor than market-related goals. A goal of cost leadership in segment B within five years can dynamise performance improvement teams. Progress within the company on unit-cost reduction can be tracked over time and compared at annual intervals with that of your competitors.

The fourth issue concerns financial goals. If the goals (or objectives) relate to segment prices or margins, whether gross margin or contribution, they can be treated in the same way as market-related goals. Motivational for the salesforce, easy to monitor.

But when they relate to the overall financial performance of the company, whether return on sales or capital, the goals may need to resolve the shareholder/stakeholder benefit trade-off. Is your firm's goal to maximise shareholder value – the so-called Anglo-Saxon business model? Or is it to achieve that only in harmony with the interests of other stakeholders, such as employees, customers, suppliers, government, community or the environment – the Continental European (or Asian) model?

Finally, your value-related goals may be just as important – see Google's goals in Figure 2.1. One such goal could be an ethical sourcing policy – for example, no child labour used by suppliers or no genetically modified cereals bought in. This is your call; though you will be aware that this may be in conflict with a goal of shareholder value maximisation.

Focus on the user and all else will follow

It's best to do one thing really, really well

Fast is better than slow

Democracy on the web works

You don't need to be at your desk to need an answer

You can make money without doing evil

There's always more information out there

The need for information crosses all borders

You can be serious without a suit

Great just isn't good enough

Figure 2.1   **An example: Google's goals**   Source: Adapted from **www.google.com**

When to use it – or be wary

You should always set long-term goals in developing strategy for your firm.

But don't have too many goals. They say people can't remember more than three of any list, but you may choose to stretch that to four or five.

Go for a dozen and you'll be lucky to attain half of them. Go for a handful and you may bag the lot.

case study

Using it: Virgin Galactic

Virgin Galactic is the commercial space arm of the Virgin Group. It aims to provide sub-orbital space tourism to all, to anyone fit – and wealthy – enough to experience the target six minutes of weightlessness in space.

Its spacecraft, SpaceShipTwo, was unveiled in December 2009 in New Mexico, and executives forecast then that the inaugural flight, lift-off from mother ship WhiteKnightTwo, would take place 'within a couple of years'.

▶ The launch date has since been postponed a number of times, leading to press speculation that it may never happen. Others are less sceptical – hundreds have already bought tickets, at $200–250,000 each, including celebs such as Brangelina.

Virgin Galactic has one long-term goal: 'To end the exclusivity attached to manned space travel, which means designing a vehicle that can fly almost anyone to space and back safely, without the need for special expertise or exhaustive, time-consuming training'.

Almost implicit in that goal is the phrase 'as long as it will take'. Proprietor Richard Branson has long said that he will be on board Virgin Galactic's maiden commercial flight.

You would be rash, or spaced out, to bet against him.

3

Setting SMART objectives

This tool will help you:

- Derive targets to aim for
- Stay on track
- Motivate management and staff

About this tool

Objectives are intimately linked to goals. Your firm aims towards a goal, a destination typically articulated in words. Objectives are targets, whether along the route or at the final destination, and typically are set out in numbers.

You may aim for the goal of national market leadership in a key segment by 2018. That is a worthy goal, but a bit too vague for a robust strategy. More precise would be the corresponding objectives of attaining 33 per cent market share by 2016 and 35 per cent by 2018. These objectives should help deliver your goal of market leadership in that segment.

How to use it

Where goals are indicative and directional, objectives are precise. You should set objectives that are:

- **Specific** – a precise number against a particular parameter
- **Measurable** – that parameter must be quantifiable – for example, a market share percentage in a segment rather than a woolly target such as 'best supplier'
- **Attainable** – there is no point in aiming for the improbable – disappointment will be the inevitable outcome
- **Relevant** – the objective should relate to the goal; if the goal is market leadership, an objective of winning 'best marketing campaign of the year' in the trade journal would be inappropriate
- **Time-limited** – you should specify by when the objective should be achieved; an objective with no time limitation would serve no motivational purpose and result in the slippage of difficult decisions.

Objectives should be SMART (see Figure 3.1). The best objectives are indeed smart. As in the example above, the objectives are: **Specific** (a market-share target in that segment), **Measurable** (market research to which you subscribe will reveal whether the 35 per cent is met), **Attainable** (you are at 29 per cent now and your new product range has been well received), **Relevant** (market share is the ultimate measure of market leadership) and **Time-limited** (2018).

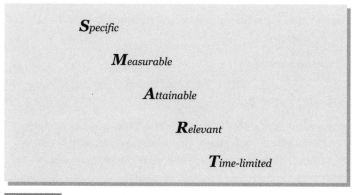

Specific

Measurable

Attainable

Relevant

Time-limited

Figure 3.1   **SMART objectives**

Here is another take on the same theme. Richard Rumelt, in his best-selling book of 2011, *Good Strategy, Bad Strategy*, states that strategy implementation is assisted greatly by the identification of 'proximate objectives'. Each of these is a target that is close enough that the firm 'can reasonably be expected to hit, or even overwhelm it'. He is emphasising the attainable 'A' component of a SMART objective.

He cites the example of President Kennedy pledging to place a man on the moon. The objective sounded fanciful, but it conveyed ambition. And Kennedy had an ace up his sleeve – he knew the technology already existed for such a mission to succeed.

When to use it – or be wary

Setting SMART objectives is an integral part of strategy development.

They are also very important in strategy implementation. Assuming key managers have been involved and brought in to the strategy development process, SMART objectives can play a key role in motivating and monitoring managerial performance during implementation.

As with goal setting, however, keep it simple. One or two objectives against each of four to five goals should be fine.

Strategy development should be underpinned by smart goals and SMART objectives.

---

case study

Using it: the BBC

The British Broadcasting Corporation has six 'public purposes', all highly commendable and indicative of the immense challenge faced by trustees and managers in keeping a formidable range of stakeholders content:

- Sustaining citizenship and civil society
- Promoting education and learning

▶ ■ Stimulating creativity and cultural excellence

■ Representing the UK, its nations, regions and communities

■ Bringing the UK to the world and the world to the UK

■ Delivering to the public the benefit of emerging communications, technologies and services.

These public purposes have led to four 'strategic objectives' during the current BBC charter period:

1 Quality and distinctiveness: all BBC services should offer high-quality content that is distinctive in terms of its creative ambition, high editorial standards and its range and depth.

2 Serving all audiences: the BBC should reflect the diversity of its audiences in both its programmes and its work force; all audiences should have access to relevant BBC services.

3 Value for money: the BBC should improve value for money and open itself to external scrutiny of this area; it should become more efficient and increase investment in content whilst reducing overheads.

4 Openness and transparency: the BBC should enable the public, and the market in which it operates, to understand how it spends its money, how it performs and what it plans to do next.

Are these objectives SMART? Let's take the first, on quality and distinctiveness:

■ Specific? Sure, it is difficult to put numbers on quality and distinctiveness, but audience surveys and focus groups might be meaningful

■ Measurable? Perhaps, as above

■ Attainable? In the absence of facts or numbers, how will we know if the objective is attained?

■ Relevant? Yes, the objective is relevant to the public purpose

■ Time-limited? Yes, this is an objective reaching until the end of the current charter period, 2016.

You guessed, some look more like goals than objectives. But we can delve deeper. If we click through on 'more on this objective' for the first ▶

► objective we find interesting information and facts on the performance of the organisation over the last few years, covering each TV and radio channel.

We learn, for example, that audience appreciation of BBC television is 'very high and continues to rise each year', with results in the Appreciation Index rising from 81.6 per cent in 2010–11 to 83.1 per cent in 2012–13.

But there is no word of the target appreciation number over the next few years. Does management aspire to 85 per cent? Is it content to hold fast at 83 per cent? Given adverse publicity concerning the former BBC disc-jockey-cum-show-host Jimmy Saville, and the pulling of an investigatory programme on him on the flagship *Newsnight* programme, would 80 per cent be a more attainable target?

We don't know. We know the BBC's goals, but not its objectives, as defined in this tool.

4

Core ideology (Collins and Porras)

This tool will help you:

- Articulate a vision for sustainable strategic success
- Set goals that both challenge and inspire
- Create a 'company' in its truest sense – a gathering of like-minded persons

About this tool

Successful companies set 'big, hairy, audacious goals'.

They also possess a core ideology and create cult-like cultures, claimed Jim Collins and Jerry I. Porras in their influential book *Built to Last: Successful Habits of Visionary Companies* in 1997.

Product lines can change – completely in some cases, such as at Nokia – leaders can change, profit can go up or down, but core ideology should remain for long-term success.

How to use it

You should break core ideology down into core purpose and core values – see Figure 4.1. Core purpose is your firm's 'fundamental reason for being'. Core values are your firm's 'essential and enduring tenets – timeless guiding principles that require no external justification'.

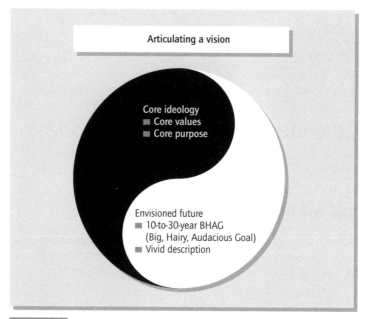

Figure 4.1   **Built to last**

Source: Adapted from James C. Collins and Jerry I. Porras, 'Building Your Company's Vision', Copyright © 1996. Reprinted by permission of Curtis Brown, Ltd.

You should set highly challenging goals, what they term big, hairy, audacious goals (BHAGs), to align ambition and enhance team spirit – viz Boeing's entry into the commercial aircraft market and President Kennedy's goal to land a man on the moon.

Visionary companies should have cult-like cultures, ones that are demanding of all employees, so much so that some, even many, might feel uncomfortable and quit. Such cultures should exhibit a fervently held ideology, mechanisms for indoctrination, procedures to ensure cultural fit and a feeling of pride, bordering on elitism.

The authors go beyond goals and objectives to identify other sources of success. One such merits highlighting, since it is in part contradictory to the purpose of this book. Successful companies never cease to innovate and test their output fast in the marketplace – see Mintzberg in Tool 20. The authors extol the virtues of continuous opportunistic experimentation, trial and error, giving ideas a quick try, but letting them die quickly if they do not work. And they deem this as preferable to strategic planning!

The authors are as stimulating on what they debunk as what they promote. In particular, they claim to disprove the notion that a great idea or a charismatic leader is needed to start a company. On the contrary, they see a core ideology and a focused leader as key to long-term success.

When to use it – or be wary

The concept of the BHAG is memorable, stimulating and can be as appropriate to the average company as it is to Boeing.

But core ideology as the cornerstone of success may seem a stretch to many smaller firms. They may see purpose and values as less crucial to successful strategy development than goals and objectives.

---

case study

Using it: Sony

Jim Collins chose the example of Sony in the 1950s as one of the most emphatic illustrations of his core ideology model.

It is hard to imagine just how poorly perceived in the West were Japanese products in those days. They were regarded as shoddy, and often with good cause.

Sony and other Japanese manufacturers in other markets, like Canon and Honda, set out to change all that. Sony's core purpose was to apply consumer technology for the benefit of the general public, worldwide.

Its core values were elevating the Japanese culture and national status, being a pioneer not a follower, and encouraging individual ability and creativity.

And it had a BHAG: to become the company at the forefront of changing the worldwide image of Japanese products.

Sony's transistor radios swept the Japanese, US and global markets, especially for teenagers. Their success was emulated in subsequent decades by the likes of the Walkman and PlayStation.

The BHAG had been scored.

The HOOF approach to demand forecasting (Evans)

This tool will help you:

- Forecast market demand in each of your key product/market segments...
- ...to a sufficient, if not great, degree of accuracy
- Tackle the market demand side of micro-economic analysis, with the next tool covering the industry supply side

About this tool

'It's better to have the wind at your back than in your face', one often hears in the business world.

It's a question of odds. You have a better chance of prospering in a market that's growing than one that's shrinking.

Market size is all very well, but what often matters more in strategy development is what the market is doing, where it is going – the dynamics, as opposed to the statics. Is market demand in your main business segments growing, shrinking or flat-lining?

This is the big question. It's not the only one, of course. Equally important, as we'll see in the next couple of chapters, is the nature of the competition you face and how you're placed to compete. But it's the first big question.

I developed, many years ago, a four-step process for translating market demand trends and drivers into forecasts. I call it the HOOF approach, for two reasons. HDDF, the strict representation of the first letters in each of the four steps, would be an unattractive, unmemorable acronym – but, with the appropriate creative licence, the circular O can be borrowed as a lookalike to the semi-circular D!

And, also, because it reminds me fondly of the junior football team I coach. No matter how many times I screech at a couple of players to play the simple ball out of defence, head up, along the ground, to a nearby player, they blindly HOOF it down the pitch with all their might, as far as their adolescent muscles can propel it!

As the ball leaves the foot, the HOOF starts the perfect trajectory of growth – the kind of market demand forecast we all would love for our business (before the ball reaches its summit and plummets to the ground, the standard path, alas, of the product life cycle).

How to use it

There are four distinct stages in the HOOF approach to demand forecasting. Get this process right and all falls logically into place. Get it out of step and you may end up with a misleading answer. You need to apply these steps for each of your main product/market segments.

The four steps are:

1 **Historic growth** – assess how market demand has grown in the past

2 **Drivers past** – identify what has been driving that past growth

3 **Drivers future** – assess whether there will be any change in influence of these and other drivers in the future

4 **Forecast growth** – forecast market demand growth, based on the influence of future drivers.

Let's look at each of these briefly, then at some examples.

1 Historic growth

This is where you need to get some facts and figures. If you have access to market research data, whether on a regular basis or with a one-off purchase, all your needs should be in there. If not, you may have to do some 'marketcrafting' – assessing the size of a market by taking your own firm's sales, estimating those of each of your major competitors, making a rough estimate for all other competitors and then doing the same exercise for three to five years beforehand, thereby enabling you to derive a very rough estimate of market growth over that period.

Be careful not to fall into the trap of relying on one recent number. Just because demand for a service jumped by, say, 8 per cent last year doesn't mean that trend growth in that market has been 8 per cent/year. The latest year may have been an aberration. The market may have dipped two years ago, remained static last year and recovered by 8 per cent this year. Average annual growth over the three years might have been only 2 per cent/year.

You should try to get an average annual (compound) growth rate over a number of recent years, preferably the last three or four. As long as there haven't been serious annual ups and downs, and there may well have been in the post-financial crisis years, usually you can get a usable approximation of average annual growth by calculating the overall percentage change in, say, the last four years and then annualising it. If there have been ups and downs, you should smooth them out with three-year moving averages before calculating the percentage change.

One word of caution: market demand growth generally is measured, analysed and forecast in real terms. You should take care to understand the differences between these growth rates:

- **In nominal terms,** that is with goods (or services) priced in the money of the day
- **In real terms,** which is the growth rate in nominal prices deflated by the growth rate in the average prices of goods in

that market; this growth rate, as long as the correct deflators are used, should be a measure of volume growth.

You should be consistent and restrict all analysis of comparative market growth rates to those in real terms in this chapter and throughout the strategy development process.

But should you need to proceed to business planning and financial forecasting, you must bring average price forecasts back into the mix. Then your revenue forecasts, as well as the whole P&L, will be able to be compared directly with market growth rate forecasts in nominal prices.

2 Drivers past

Once you have uncovered some information on recent market demand growth, find out what has been influencing that growth. Typical factors that influence demand in many markets are:

- Per capita income growth
- Population growth in general
- Population growth specific to a market (for example, of pensioners or baby boomers, or general population growth in a particular area)
- Some aspect of government policy or purchasing
- Changing awareness, perhaps from high levels of promotion by competing providers
- Business structural shifts (such as toward outsourcing)
- Price change
- Fashion, even a craze
- Weather – seasonal variations, but maybe even the longer-term effects of climate change.

Or your sector may be heavily influenced by demand in other sectors, typically customer sectors. Thus the demand for steel is heavily dependent on demand for automobiles, ships, capital goods equipment and construction. Demand for automobiles is also the major driver for demand for Tier 1 car-seat suppliers, which in turn drives demand for Tier 2 steel seat-reclining mechanism suppliers, who in turn buy from specialist steel producers.

A vertical sector relationship may be so close that you may be able to obtain sound estimates of derived demand. You can obtain excellent automotive market forecasts from specialist market research companies, thereby guiding Tier 2 suppliers like seat-mechanism producers in their forecasts.

But be careful of derived demand forecasts – there are always **other** drivers. The average number of seats per car sold may be changing due to the popularity of 4×4s. A major car company may decide to opt for an alternative car-seat technology.

The same applies in deriving demand forecasts from those in complementary or related sectors. Thus demand growth for accommodation in 3-star hotels in the English West Country will be influenced by demand growth for coach package tours, but it will not be the same. The latter will not be the only driver of the former. Another driver is the sterling-euro exchange rate, which will be a major influence on whether cost-conscious coach travellers from the North of England opt for destinations in the West Country, France or further afield.

3 Drivers future

Now you need to assess how each of these drivers is likely to develop over the next few years. Are things going to carry on more or less as before for a driver? Or are things going to change significantly?

For instance, will immigration continue to drive local population growth? Is the Government likely to hike up a local tax? Could this market become less fashionable?

What are the prospects for growth in vertical or complementary sectors?

The most important driver is, of course, the economic cycle. If it seems the economy is poised for a nosedive, that could have a serious impact on demand in your business over the next year or two – assuming your business is relatively sensitive (or 'elastic', in economics-speak) to the economic cycle. Or maybe your business is relatively inelastic, like, for example, in much of the food industry? You may need to think carefully about the timing of the economic cycle and the elasticity of your business.

4 Forecast growth

This is the fun bit. You've assembled all the information on past trends and drivers. Now you can weave it all together, sprinkle it with a large dose of judgement, and you have a forecast of market demand – not without risk, not without uncertainty, but a systematically derived forecast nevertheless.

Let's take a simple example of the HOOF approach in action. In one of your business segments, your firm offers a relatively new service to the elderly. Step 1 (**H**): You find that the market has been growing at 5–10 per cent per year over the last few years. Step 2 (**O**): You identify the main drivers as (a) per capita income growth, (b) growth in the elderly population, and (c) growing awareness of the service by elderly people. Step 3 (**O**): You believe income growth will continue as before, the elderly population will grow even faster in the future, and that awareness can get only more widespread. Step 4 (**F**): You conclude that growth in your market will accelerate and could reach over 10 per cent per year over the next few years.

The HOOF approach is best used diagrammatically. The example above is simple, but becomes even simpler when displayed on a diagram – see Figure 5.1. The impact of each demand driver on demand growth is represented by varying numbers of plus and minus signs, or a zero. In this case you can see that there will be more pluses in the near future than there were in the past, implying that demand growth **will accelerate** – from the historic 5–10 per cent/year to the future 10 per cent/year plus.

In real-world strategy development, there will be more such charts, one for each key product/market segment, and each will have more drivers. But the fundamental principles of the HOOF

Demand drivers for a new service in the US to the elderly	Impact on demand growth			Comments
	Recent past	Now	Next few years	
Growth in incomes	-	0	+	■ US to resume economic growth, assuming no double-dip
Growth in elderly population	++	+	++	■ Proportion of US population aged 65+ forecast to grow from 13% to 18.5% by 2025 (US Census Bureau)
Increased awareness of service	+++	++	+++	■ Newspaper coverage, national and local, greater all the time
Overall impact	+	+	++	
Market growth rate	5 to 10%/yr	5 to 10%	Over 10%/yr	

H   O   O   F

Key to driver impact
+++ Very strong positive
++ Strong positive
+ Some positive
0 None
– Some negative
– – Strong negative
– – – Very strong negative

Figure 5.1 The HOOF approach to demand forecasting: an example

approach will remain. The chart will show the historic growth rate (H), identify the relative impact of drivers past and future (O & O) and conclude with a growth forecast for that segment (F).

And now for an example of how not to do it. Many years ago I was doing some work for a crane manufacturer in the North of England and came across a draft business plan. In the section on market demand, its young author had stated there was no data on UK demand for cranes to be found anywhere. So, for the purposes of the financial forecasts, he assessed real growth in the crane market to be the same as for UK engineering output, forecast then by OECD at 2.4 per cent/year.

Oops! The mistake was one of exclusion. Yes, macro-economic demand was an important driver of demand in the crane market, as for all engineering output. But there were three or four other drivers of as great importance, on which there was, admittedly, no hard and fast data, but plenty of anecdotal evidence. They included evidence of crane destocking, a thriving second-hand market and, above all, an imminent downturn in high-rise construction activity.

None of these drivers bore any relation to engineering output as a whole and their combined impact served to translate a 2.4 per cent/year crane market growth forecast into one of steep decline, possibly at 10 per cent/year for two or three years.

The moral of the tale is to make sure **all** drivers are taken into account, **irrespective of whether hard data can be found on them**. The HOOF process encourages you to seek out all relevant drivers and assess their influence in a structured, combined quantitative and qualitative context.

When to use it – or be wary

Use the HOOF approach whenever you need to forecast demand in a key product/market segment.

If your firm is large and addresses primarily sizeable segments, you may not need to use the HOOF approach. There may be half a dozen reputable market research companies who are all over your market. Given the direct access that they often get to the leading individuals in the market, both industry players and major customers, their findings should be more authoritative than anything you can do for yourself.

But it is always worth checking to make sure that the market research reports use an approach similar to that of the HOOF approach in their forecasts. The quality can be variable. Some take shortcuts.

If yours is a small to medium-sized firm, however, it is unlikely that market research reports will be disaggregated sufficiently to be of direct use to your demand forecasts. Even in a large firm, you may well struggle to find market research reports on a segment large to you but small in the market, or on a new segment you are moving into.

In which case, the HOOF approach is the tool for you to forecast demand.

And remember: take care to identify all the relevant drivers. Use whatever evidence you can muster, dashed by a strong dose of reasoned judgement, in assessing their influence on demand growth, past, present and future.

---

case study

Using it: Apps

In the mid-2000s the word 'app' was in the preserve of techies. To laypeople, it was as likely to refer to an apprenticeship or an appendix as to an application. Today, thanks to its extension from web apps to mobile apps, it is ubiquitous – encompassing a market worth $25 billion.

The mobile app market has been an electronic gold rush. Not only have big companies piled into the rush, but so too have thousands of little guys – some of whom, like Instagram, have become big, and done so fast. But, as in any gold rush, most have foundered and seen little return on their endeavours.

▶ Created by Apple, followed aggressively by Google, and courted by Microsoft, Blackberry and Amazon in the USA, the mobile app came from nowhere. Originally focused on basic business needs, like e-mail, stock reports and weather, they piggybacked on smartphones into bandwidth-intensive areas such as games and global satellite positioning.

Market growth has been exponential. Think Angry Birds – or, later, Flappy Birds. It remains rapid – over 60 per cent in 2013. But, as in any product life cycle, the app market surely will follow the standard growth path, from the embryonic and growth stages into those of maturity and decline. The trick for the forecaster is to know when and how fast growth will tail off.

Main demand drivers include smartphone penetration, real personal disposable income growth, the number of app stores, the number of app developers, the development of high-profile, successful apps, extension to tablets, laptops and televisions, the relative cost of app maintenance to app development, consumer acceptance of revenue-raising methods such as advertising, premium service and packaging with other services, unit advertising costs and promotional spend on apps. As the relative impact and weight of these drivers change, so too will the market growth rates.

There is plenty of growth yet to come – but it won't be quite as app-oplectic as in recent years.

The five forces (Porter)

This tool will help you:

- Tackle the industry supply side of micro-economic analysis, with the previous tool covering the market demand side

- Provide an analytical framework for assessing competitive intensity in each of your key product/market segments

- Be guided in gauging industry pricing and profitability in the future

About this tool

Competitive intensity determines industry profitability.

That is the basic premise of Michael Porter's work. And he went on to describe in detail what the fundamental forces are that drive competitive intensity.

His five forces model made its first appearance beyond a Harvard Business School lecture theatre in his *Competitive Strategy: Techniques for Analyzing Industries and Competitors* in 1980. It has remained the pre-eminent tool in the analysis of industry supply ever since.

He set out to show that firms in any industry were constrained from maximising profit not just by rivalry with their competitors but by four further competitive forces. These five forces shape competitive intensity:

1 Internal rivalry

2 Threat of new entrants

3 Ease of substitution

4 Customer power

5 Supplier power.

Porter showed how these five forces impact on competitive intensity by means of a simple, memorable diagram – see Figure 6.1.

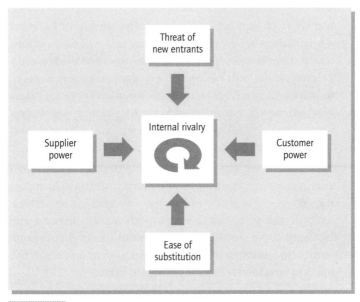

Figure 6.1   **Five forces shaping competition**

Source: Adapted with the permission of Simon & Schuster Publishing Group from the Free Press edition of *COMPETITIVE STRATEGY: Techniques for Analyzing Industries and Competitors* by Michael E. Porter. Copyright (c) 1980 1998 by The Free Press. All rights reserved.

How to use it

Each of the five forces is, in turn, driven by a number of sub-forces and factors, and is examined briefly below.

1 Internal rivalry

Internal rivalry is shaped by three main sub-forces: the number of players, market demand growth relative to supply, and external pressures.

1 **The number of players.** The more numerous the players, the tougher, typically, the competition.

2 **Market demand growth.** The slower growing the market, the tougher, typically, the competition.

   And what of supply? Are demand and supply in balance? Where there is balance, internal rivalry may well be moderate. Where there is oversupply – where supply exceeds demand – internal rivalry will be intensified. And a dampener placed on prices. Conversely, where there is undersupply (or excess demand), where customers compete for relatively scarce supplies, internal rivalry will be modest – and you and your competitors may be able to nudge up pricing above inflation.

3 **External pressures.** External bodies, in particular government and the trade unions, have great power to influence the nature of competition in many industries. Government regulation, taxation and subsidies can skew both market demand and the competitive landscape. Trade unions can influence competition in a number of ways, for example through restrictive practices which serve to raise barriers to entry.

There are other, lesser factors influencing internal rivalry. Barriers to exit are one such. Where providers have little choice but to stay on competing when they should be withdrawing (for example, a restaurant with many employees, hence potentially high redundancy costs, or a service business with a long lease on office space which is difficult to offload), competition is intensified. Low barriers to exit, such as the minicab business, reduce internal rivalry.

Seasonal or irregular overcapacity is another factor. Fluctuating levels of demand (for example, the fruit picking or ice cream industries) intensify competition.

2 Threat of new entrants

The lower the barriers to entry to a market, the tougher, typically, the competition. Barriers to entry can be technology, operations, people or cost-related, where a new entrant has to:

- develop or acquire a certain technology
- develop or acquire a certain operational process
- gain access to a limited distribution channel
- train or engage scarce personnel
- invest heavily in either capital assets or marketing to become a credible provider.

Switching costs also influence entry barriers. The higher the costs to the customer of switching from one supplier to another the higher are the entry barriers. A drinks manufacturer may shift from one sugar supplier to another with relative ease, but may require redesign of the factory in switching from one labelling solution to another.

3 Ease of substitution

The easier it is for customers to use a substitute product or service, the tougher, typically, the competition.

Consider the impact of the likes of iTunes in the music industry. It was a substitute solution to the sale of CDs in the high street and a contributory factor, along with e-commerce and the supermarkets, to the demise of retailers such as Woolworths and Zavvi.

4 Customer power

The more bargaining power customers possess, the tougher, typically, the competition. Ask any supplier to the supermarket chains. Or to automotive manufacturers.

Often this is no more than a reflection of the number of providers in a marketplace, compared with the number of customers. The more choice of provider the customer has, the tougher the competition.

Customer power is also influenced by switching costs. If it's easy and relatively painless to switch supplier, competition is tougher. If switching costs are high, competition abates.

5 Supplier power

The more bargaining power suppliers possess, the tougher, typically, the competition.

Again, it can be just a function of numbers. There are, for example, numerous steel or aluminium converters, but few, and increasingly fewer, metal producers. When metal converters sell components to automotive manufacturers, they can find themselves in a vice-like squeeze: huge steel or aluminium suppliers at one end, auto giant customers at the other. But the best of them learn how to duck, dive and survive.

Overall competitive intensity

These are the five main forces shaping the degree of competition in a marketplace. Put them all together, and you'll have a measure of how competitive your industry is.

In some industries, such as soft drinks, software, toiletries, all five forces operate benignly to boost profitability – and consistently over the decades. In other industries, like airlines or textiles, the opposite is true – all five forces act against the airlines and average profitability over the years is dreadful.

How tough is internal rivalry in your industry? And the threat of new entrants or substitutes? How much power do customers and suppliers have over you and your competitors? In short, how intense is competition in your industry? High, low, medium? Or somewhere in between?

And what of the future? Is industry competition set to intensify? Because, however tough it is at the moment, it results in you and your competitors getting an average operating margin of a certain per cent.

But will competitive forces conspire to threaten that margin over the next few years? Or has the industry competition of the last few years been unsustainable and likely to ease off in the future?

In short, what will be the effect of competitive dynamics on pricing in your industry over the next few years?

Will competition intensify and put pressure on prices? Will it stay more or less as is and pricing move as it has been doing in recent times? Or will competition ease off, enabling players to nudge up pricing over the next few years?

When to use it – or be wary

I cannot recall a strategy assignment when I did not deploy this tool. It is an essential arrow in the strategist's quiver.

But it has had its critics over the years. Some believe that boundary definition – this activity is part of the industry you operate in, that activity is not – can, in itself, place strategy development in a straitjacket. Pioneering companies succeed by redefining industry boundaries – see, for example, blue ocean strategy, Tool 15.

This critique can often be addressed by further segmentation – by returning to Tool 1 and redefining key product/market segments to allow for shifting boundaries.

Other critics have promoted the corporate environment (government, the regulatory framework, pressure groups, etc.) as a sixth force, while still others believe that complements, as distinct from substitutes, should be a separate and sixth force.

These are valid points, but to an extent industry-specific, with some industries more affected by such forces than others. Porter himself recognises the influence of these forces, but incorporates them effectively as sub-forces to his five main forces.

Kevin Coyne and Somu Subramaniam challenged Porter's model in 2001 on three grounds. They questioned these assumptions:

- An industry consists of a set of unrelated buyers, sellers, substitutes and competitors that interact at arm's length – with little allowance made for codependent systems, such as strategic alliances, networks and webs, or privileged relationships, whether based on financial interest, friendship, trust or ethnic loyalty.

- Wealth will accrue to companies that erect barriers against competitors and potential entrants, in other words the source of value is structural advantage – with little allowance made for management, whether through frontline execution or insight/foresight.

- Uncertainty is low, allowing the prediction of competitive response and contingency planning – with little allowance made for differing degrees of uncertainty, ranging from the structural, where the model may be valid, through alternative scenarios and continuous uncertainty to complete ambiguity, where the model is invalid.

The authors make valid points, and the first bullet, especially, needs to be borne in mind in industry analysis. But they offer a revised industry model, reinforced by a risk-adjusted situation analysis, which is so complex that they fail to spot the true genius of Porter's model. It is a starting point for industry analysis and strategy development, not the end point. Its simplicity is its overriding virtue.

Finally, Porter's model has taken some hits from those who point out, conclusively, as in the second bullet above, that industry structure alone tends to be insufficient to explain differences in profitability. Richard Rumelt, for example, in a 1991 study, found that differences in firms' profitability can be attributed much more to specific 'firm effects' (44 per cent) than to 'industry effects' (4 per cent). (Incidentally, the unexplained variance was 45 per cent.) Other studies have shown likewise.

But this does not invalidate the model. Industry analysis is part of the strategy story and Porter's Five Forces model a very large part of industry analysis. It is not the final word, but arguably the most critical tool in a strategy development toolkit.

case study

Using it: Blockbuster

There are times when all of Porter's five forces seem to conspire against an industry sector. Just ask Blockbuster.

At its peak in the mid-2000s, Blockbuster had over 4,000 video/DVD/ game rental shops throughout the USA, employing over 60,000 people. It was also the largest such chain in Canada and the UK and had operations in 17 countries. By the time it filed for Chapter 11 bankruptcy in September 2010, only 700 stores were still trading in the USA. What had gone wrong?

The industry had moved on. As for its main competitor, Movie Gallery Inc. (with Hollywood Video and Game Crazy), which preceded Blockbuster by three years into bankruptcy, the five forces were arraigned against them:

- Industry rivalry (1) had intensified due to dampened demand, caused by:
    - new entrants (2) that focused on alternative, consumer-friendly distribution methods, in particular by post (Netflix, with less demanding return requirements) and pick-up kiosks (Redbox)
    - substitute products, (3) especially video on-demand services from streaming over the Internet (Netflix again, far ahead of Blockbuster's own streaming product).
- Meanwhile consumers (4) have become savvier and able to select from a wider variety of competing offerings for movies, television and games, thereby putting pressure on pricing.
- Suppliers (5) were becoming more demanding, as the bargaining power of the bricks and mortar movie and game rental chains waned.

Blockbuster was bought at auction by Dish Network, the satellite television service provider. Dish resolved to deploy the Blockbuster brand to compete directly with Netflix and to keep 90 per cent of stores open. These plans seemed highly optimistic and, indeed, were soon scaled back to retaining only the most profitable branches. Two years later, however, it was with a sense of inevitability, given the mal-alignment of the five forces against it, that Dish announced the closure of all remaining Blockbuster stores.

Progress was blocked, the chain busted.

7

Rating competitive position

This tool will help you:

- Rate your firm's performance against the key success factors in each main segment
- Assess how well positioned your firm is in each segment
- Target the strategic gap between where you are today and where you should aim to be in the future

About this tool

'A man can't be too careful in the choice of his enemies', said Oscar Wilde. So, too, perhaps, with firms and their choice of where and with whom to compete.

With whom have you chosen to compete? And how do you rate against them?

How is your overall competitive position? And theirs? How do your relative positions differ by product/market segment?

In this tool you will rate your competitive position against each key competitor, over time and for each main segment.

You could do this right now, at your desk, based on feedback you and your sales and purchasing teams have received from customers and suppliers over the years. Or you could do it more methodically, via a structured interviewing programme, primarily of customers.

In this analysis you will assess your strengths and weaknesses and those of your peers. It will pinpoint your source of competitive advantage – as well as that of your most formidable competitor.

How to use it

There are three stages in rating competitive position and you should follow these for each of your firm's main product/market segments:

1 Identify and weight customer purchasing criteria (CPCs) – what customers need from their suppliers in each segment, that is you and your competitors

2 Derive and weight key success factors (KSFs) – what you and your competitors need to do to satisfy these customer needs and run a successful business

3 Rate your competitive position – how you rate against those key success factors relative to your competitors.

We'll assume, for the purposes of this book, that you have already undertaken the first two stages and have derived and weighted KSFs for each of your main product/market segments – either methodically or using your business judgement. As a check, you might choose to take a quick look at Tools 23 and 24 in this book's more comprehensive partner, *Key Strategy Tools*, where the processes for identifying CPCs and deriving KSFs are set out in detail.

The process of rating competitive position is straightforward. Use a 0–5 rating system. If you perform about the same as your peers against a KSF, give yourself a score in the middle, a 3 (good, favourable). If you perform very strongly, even dominantly, a 5 (very strong). Poorly, a 1 (weak). If you perform not quite as well as most others, give yourself a 2 (tenable). Better than most, a 4 (strong).

Now do the same for each of your competitors against that KSF. Who's the best performer against this KSF? Do they merit a 5, or are they better but not **that** much better than others, for a 4?

And so on against each KSF.

If you've used Excel, your competitive position literally falls out at the bottom of the spreadsheet. Your overall rating is the sum of each rating (r) against each KSF, multiplied by the percentage weighting (w) of the KSF. If there are n KSFs, your overall rating will be **(r1 * w1) + (r2 * w2) + (r3 * w3) + ... + (rn * wn)**. As long as the percentage weightings add up to 100 per cent, you should get the right answer.

Figure 7.1 gives an example, one adapted from a recent strategy assignment. It shows that the company was the leading player in its niche UK engineering market, but there was no room for complacency. The company had the largest presence in the market,

Key success factors in UK engineering niche market	Weighting	The company	Competitor A	Competitor B
Market share	15%	5	3.3	2
Cost factors	35%	4	3.5	2.5
Differentiation factors: Product capability and range	15%	4	4.5	3
Product reliability	15%	4	4	2.5
Engineering service network	10%	5	3.5	2.5
Customer service	10%	3	3	2
Competitive position	100%	4.2	3.6	2.5

Key: 1 = Weak, 2 = Tenable, 3 = Favourable, 4 = Strong, 5 = Dominant

Figure 7.1   Competitive position: an example

the best engineering service network and a strong cost base, but competitor A had developed a product with enhanced features and functionality that was proving attractive to customers.

Competing by segment

Apply the same process for each key product/market segment: identifying how customer purchasing criteria differ by segment, assessing key success factors for each and deriving competitive position in each. You'll find that some positions will vary due to weighting. Take product quality. Your rating against that KSF may well be the same in each segment relating to a product group. But its weighting may differ by customer group segment, thereby impacting your overall competitive position in each.

Ratings for the same KSF may well differ by segment. For instance, your company may have an enviable track record in service and repair in one segment, but you haven't been in another long – rating a 5 in the first, but only a 2 in the other. Again, that will filter down to the bottom line of competitive position.

Competing over time

So far your analysis of competitive position has been static. You've rated your firm's current competitiveness and those of others. But that's only the first part of the story. How has your competitive position changed over the last few years and how is it likely to change over the next few years? You need to understand the dynamics. Is it set to improve or worsen?

The simplest way to do this is to add an extra column to your chart, representing your position in, say, three years' time. Then you can build in any improvements in your ratings against each KSF. These prospective improvements need, for the time being, to be both in the pipeline **and** likely. In the next chapter we shall assess how you can **proactively and systematically** improve your competitive position. That's strategy. But, for now, it is useful to see how your competitive position seems set to evolve naturally over the next few years, assuming no significant change in strategy.

Remember, however, that improved competitive position is a two-edged sword. Your competitors, too, will have plans. This is where analysis of KSF dynamics gets challenging. It's easy enough to know what you're planning, but what are your competitors up to?

Try adding a couple of further columns representing your two most fearsome competitors as they may be in three years' time. Do you have any idea what they're planning to do to improve their competitiveness in the near future? What are they likely to do? What could they do? **What are you afraid they'll do?**

Returning to the example of the UK niche engineering company, management was aware that competitor A had plans to outsource certain components and reduce cost and set up a joint venture to enhance its engineering service capability. A's strategy seemed set to narrow the competitive gap unless my client deployed a proactive strategy focusing on R&D – see Figure 7.2.

Key success factors in UK engineering niche market	Weighting	The company	Competitor A today	Competitor A tomorrow
Market share	15%	5	3.3	2
Cost factors	35%	4	3.5	2.5
Differentiation factors: Product capability and range	15%	4	4.5	3
Product reliability	15%	4	4	2.5
Engineering service network	10%	5	3.5	2.5
Customer service	10%	3	3	2
Competitive position	100%	4.2	3.6	4.0

Key: 1 = Weak, 2 = Tenable, 3 = Favourable, 4 = Strong, 5 = Dominant

Figure 7.2   Future competitive position: an example

Getting past first base

There is one type of KSF to which you should pay special attention – the must-have KSF, in which, without a good rating, your
business cannot even begin to compete.

Is there a must-have KSF in any of your business segments? If so,
how do you rate against it? Favourable? Strong? Fine. Okay-ish?
Questionable. Weak? Troublesome. A straight zero, not even a 1?
You're out. You don't get past first base.

And what about in a few years' time? Could any KSF develop into
a must-have? How will you rate then? Will you get past first base?

And, even though you rate as tenable against a must-have KSF
today, might it slip over time? Could it slide below 2, into tricky
territory?

This may be a case of being cruel to be kind. It's better to know.
The sooner you realise that you're in a wrong business segment,
the sooner you can withdraw and focus resources on the right
segments.

Implications for future market share

This tool plays a useful role in business planning. It gives you an
idea of how your firm is likely to fare over the next few years **in
relation to the market as a whole**.

If your overall competitive position turns out to be around 3, or
good/favourable, you should, other things being equal, be able to
grow business **in line with the market** over the next few years. In
other words, to hold market share.

If it is around 4 or above, you should be able to **beat the market**,
to gain market share, again, other things being equal. Suppose
you forecast market demand growth of 10 per cent a year. With a
competitive position of 4, you should feel comfortable that you
can grow your business at, say, 12–15 per cent a year.

If your competitive position is around 2, however, you'll be less
confident about your business prospects. It's more likely you'll

underperform the market and, if your boss is expecting the firm to outpace the market, something will have to change!

Implications for strategy development

This tool throws up some facts and judgements that are highly useful for strategy development:

- How you compete overall in key segments – hence where you are most likely to be most profitable relative to the competition
- Areas of strength in key segments that can be built on
- Areas of weakness in some segments that may need to be worked on
- Areas of strength or weakness, common to many or all segments, that can be built on or worked on to benefit across the board
- Relative competitiveness in each key segment
- Change in competitiveness over time
- In summary, your source of competitive advantage, tracked over time.

This tool forms the basis for identification of the strategic gap, to be targeted and bridged later in the strategy development process.

When to use it – or be wary

Rating competitive position is an integral part of strategy development.

But, having used this tool for three decades and managed many junior consultants in its use, I have identified three areas where you may need to take care:

1   Too much analysis hinders decision making – don't apply this tool to too many segments, too many KSFs, too many competitors within each segment or too many years past and future; keep it simple – opt for the main segments, the main KSFs, the

main competitors, now and three years' hence; look for the main findings, the key lessons; drill down further only if necessary and potentially illuminating.

2   Don't get too scientific – stick to the nearest whole number in the 0–5 range or, when you are torn between a 3 and a 4, go for a 3.5; the exception is for market share, which lends itself to more precise, proportionate quantification – if competitor A has 60 per cent share, B 25 per cent and C 15 per cent, don't give A a 5, B a 3 and C a 1, be more precise; keep A at 5 and give B a 2.1 and C a 1.2.

3   Always have a first shot with or without the relevant research, but, if you feel uncomfortable about a rating, type it provisionally into Excel in red or in italics and undertake to do the required research before firming up the rating.

Circumnavigate these pitfalls and the tool is invaluable.

---

case study

Using it: Samuel Adams

Charles Koch was a fifth generation brewer. Koch beers had been brewed in St Louis, Missouri since the mid-19th century, barring a hiccup during the prohibition era. But it looked like his son Jim would be anything but a brewer, with the Harvard graduate opting for a career in management consulting. Beer, however, was in the blood and he kept one eye on what was happening in the industry.

Jim noted that the US beer industry of the early 1980s offered virtually no variety. The likes of Budweiser, Busch, Schaefer, Schlitz, Miller, Michelob, Coors and Molson were all pale lagers, manufactured by large, mass-market breweries. Pale lagers, derided as insipid by European visitors accustomed to a fruitier taste, were clearly the preference of most Americans. But if they wanted a beer with a bit more flavour, they had to drink an imported Heineken or Beck's – or indeed, at the other extreme to a pale lager, a British ale.

Jim believed that the US consumer wanted more choice, to try something different. He dusted off a recipe from his great-great-grandfather's records and tried brewing it in his Boston kitchen. Father Charles thought him crazy, especially when Jim quit his consulting group to take on the venture full time. But Jim pressed on. He named his beer inspirationally after the Bostonian revolutionary, Samuel Adams, who was himself a brewer, and carted his sample bottles around the bars and restaurants of Boston.

Samuel Adams Boston Lager made its debut in around 25 Boston venues in April 1985, produced by a company with no office, no computers, no distributors and just two employees – Jim and his partner. By the end of the year, sales had reached 500 barrels and word was spreading. In 1988 a small brewery was built and 36,000 barrels sold.

Sam Adams is a classic example of differentiation strategy. All the big guys were producing pale lagers, with differences, yes, in packaging, advertising, price positioning and, mildly, flavour. But each was, essentially, a pale lager. Sam Adams, on the other hand, was a malt-flavoured, 'better' beer.

The differentiation strategy worked. Many new lines followed the original Sam Adams and distribution became both nationwide and international. Parent company Boston Beer was to pioneer a micro-brewery explosion throughout the USA. It now has sales of over $500 million and, following the $52 billion takeover of Anheuser-Busch by the Belgian/Brazilian Inbev in 2008, is now, remarkably, the largest US-owned brewer.

Jim had rolled out the barrel.

The resource and capability strengths/importance matrix (Grant)

This tool will help you:

- Identify the resources and capabilities needed for success in your business
- Assess whether these are areas of strength for your firm
- Pinpoint where further investment should be directed

About this tool

How strategically important is whatever your firm does well?

Rob Grant's essential tool puts your firm's resources and capabilities into perspective. It assesses them by two criteria – how important they are relative to each other and how strongly you are placed relative to the competition.

You should start by differentiating between your firm's resources and capabilities. Resources are the productive assets owned by the firm, whether tangible, intangible or human. Capabilities are what the firm does with its resources, how it deploys them.

Land, buildings, plant and equipment are resources. So, too, are intangible resources such as brand and personnel. How they work together organisationally and operationally, whether in production, purchasing, product development, sales or marketing, are the firm's capabilities.

This tool is more relevant for looking at your business as a whole, the strategic business unit, as opposed to the previous tool's drilling down into each key product/market segment. It can also be used in corporate strategy, analysing the shared resources and capabilities of the centre as well as of each business unit.

How to use it

Grant offers a three-step approach on appraising resources and capabilities and thereby guiding strategy development:

1   Identify key resources and capabilities
2   Appraise them
     - Assess their relative importance
     - Assess your relative strengths
     - Bring the appraisal together
3   Develop strategy implications.

In the first step, you need to translate the key success factors you assessed in the previous tool into specific resources and capabilities. For this, value chain analysis (the next tool) may also be of help.

Then you rate them by degree of importance, as defined by which resources or capabilities are the more important in conferring competitive advantage.

Next you assess how your firm stacks up versus the competition in each of these resources and capabilities – as you did in the previous tool. Here, you may find a benchmarking exercise helpful, whereby you measure key metrics in the operations, systems and processes in your firm against best practice, whether in your industry or elsewhere.

This leads us to the strengths/importance matrix, a simple but most revealing chart – see Figure 8.1. Here you can appraise your firm's strengths and weaknesses visually in the context of their strategic importance.

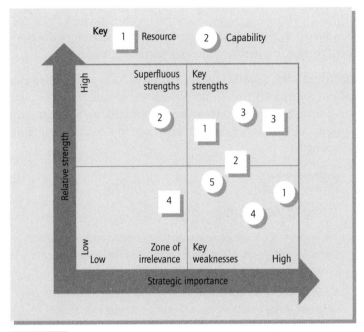

Figure 8.1   **The resource strengths/importance matrix**

Source: Adapted from Robert M. Grant,
Contemporary Strategy Analysis, Blackwell, 7th edition, 2011

Resources and capabilities that appear in the top right quadrant are very good news and suggest competitive advantage. Those in the bottom right quadrant are of concern – your firm is potentially weak in those resources or capabilities deemed of strategic importance.

Those in the top left quadrant are superfluous (you're strong in unimportant areas) and in the bottom left irrelevant (you're weak in unimportant areas).

Finally, you can develop the strategic implications of the process. How can you exploit the key strengths displayed – perhaps by further targeted investment in developing capabilities? How can you manage the key weaknesses – perhaps through outsourcing? To what extent can the superfluous strengths be deployed to greater effect on shareholder value – perhaps through divestment?

When to use it – or be wary

This matrix is another critical component of a strategy development process, invariably yielding penetrating insights.

But the strategic implications need care. Successful companies are not necessarily those that possess the greater resources, but those that leverage them (Hamel and Prahalad, see Tool 19). And working on weaknesses may not give as good a return as building on strengths.

---

case study

Using it: Virgin Group

We looked at the Virgin Group earlier, or rather one of its subsidiaries, Virgin Galactic, in the setting of long-term goals. Now let's look at the group itself.

Virgin Group is a highly diversified company or, rather, a holding group of various equity participations, in scores of businesses – in lifestyle, media and mobile, money, music and travel. Is it a conglomerate, along the lines of Hanson and Tomkins of the 1970s, or does it have some unifying coherence?

Does it possess distinct, value-adding, reinforceable core resources or capabilities?

Virgin Atlantic provides the clue. It has survived, against all the odds, for a number of reasons, but one stands out: an extraordinary brand name – a name associated not just with quality, value-for-money service, but also with a man-of-the-people – David fighting against a global Goliath. All brushed with more than a hint of glamour and excitement. And Branson raised this image to new heights following the airline launch, embarking personally on a series of world speed record attempts to keep the brand affixed to the headlines.

Buoyed by this unique and unprecedented corporate branding, Branson's airline has succeeded. It has held its own both with British Airways and with US transatlantic carriers. It has survived two severe downturns in the air industry without government subsidisation or recourse to Chapter 11 bankruptcy.

The brand and the customer benefits it conveys are the secret to Virgin Group's success. It applies across the group, from Virgin Active to Virgin Books, Virgin Media to Virgin Money – even to Virgin Trains, which at one stage threatened to tarnish the brand but has persevered, investing in sleek, fast, tilting trains.

The brand is now being extended to the space tourism business. Virgin Galactic not only benefits from the glamour of the Virgin brand but sends it into orbit.

The value chain (Porter)

This tool will help you:

- Divide your business into activities, whether primary or support
- Pinpoint the sources of value creation in your firm
- Identify opportunities to further augment value

About this tool

'You are the weakest link' has entered the realms of memorable, if shrill and irritating, catch phrases. But are there weak links in your business?

The value chain is a tool for identifying key processes in your business, assessing your firm's competitive capabilities in each and thereby assessing wherein lies the source of your competitive advantage.

It was first introduced by Michael Porter in 1984 and, as with his Five Forces model (Tool 6), has withstood robustly the test of time.

How to use it

Porter divides a firm's activities into primary and support activities – see Figure 9.1. Primary activities involve the conversion of a range of inputs to the production process through to the delivery of the output to the customer and beyond. Or, in the case of a service business, they involve the conversion of personnel and their work tools through the operational processes to service delivery and after-sales service.

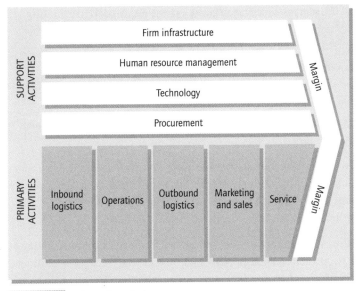

Figure 9.1　**The value chain**

Source: Adapted from Michael E. Porter, *Competitive Strategy: Techniques for Analyzing Industries and Competitors*, Free Press, 1980

Primary activities are:

- **Inbound logistics** – those required to receive, store and disseminate inputs
- **Operations** – those required to transform inputs into outputs
- **Outbound logistics** – those required to collect, store and distribute the output
- **Marketing and sales** – those required to generate awareness of the firm's outputs and their benefits and to stimulate customers to buy them
- **Service** – those required to maintain effective working of the product or service post-sale.

Support activities are those that apply across the range of primary activities. They are:

- **The firm's infrastructure** – those required to serve the firm's general needs, typically centred on HQ, such as accounting, finance, legal, planning, PR and general management
- **Human resource management** – those required to recruit, hire, train, develop, compensate and (as necessary) discipline or dismiss personnel
- **Technology** – those required to research and develop the equipment, hardware, software and processes needed in all primary activities
- **Procurement** – those required to acquire inputs needed in all primary activities.

Note that Porter takes technology and procurement as support activities, not primary. In practice, they can be treated as primary activities as long as you recognise that they can be applicable to other such activities.

Thus you can replace technology with information technology as a support activity and insert R&D as a primary activity – or indeed split it into two, product R&D and production R&D. It is up to you – think what will be most illuminating for your business in terms of identifying key success factors.

Procurement used to be treated often as a primary activity, since the term used to be virtually synonymous with the purchasing of raw materials and components. This is no longer the case. The spread of outsourcing and offshoring in the 1990s has meant that procurement activities now can be equally important in operations, even in outbound logistics or post-sale service.

Having identified the primary and support activities in your business, you need to assess which of them, or which sub-activities within them, are creating the real value in your firm and to what extent they are inter-linked in the chain.

Finally, what opportunities emerge from the value chain analysis that may yield further value creation?

When to use it – or be wary

You should use value chain analysis when you need to clarify which activities are most important to your business success – in other words, which activities are KSFs and how you can improve your capabilities in them.

This is a tool best deployed across the whole business, or strategic business unit. Given that activities such as human resource management or procurement are likely to be common to all product/ market segments, it is seldom appropriate to use value chain analysis for a specific segment.

---

case study

Using it: Zara

The savvy woman doesn't think twice when she shops in Zara. If she likes it, she buys it, there and then. She may not see that garment on display again.

Zara's model has revolutionised the women's fashion world. It has turned the value chain on its head. The industry standard model is, for each season, design the range, manufacture (typically in a least-cost location), ship, display, market, discount in the end-of-season sale and repeat for the next season.

Zara, from its space-age command HQ and vast warehouses in Galicia, North-western Spain, does things differently.

Founder Amancio Ortega likens selling fashion to selling fish. If it's fresh, it commands a premium price. If it's yesterday's catch, the price plummets.

Trends and styles change continuously at Zara, even by the day. There is always something new for the shopper to see on display.

Manufacturing, mainly from Spain, is in small batches and the output tested in the marketplace. Results are fed back to HQ. They know what is selling and what is not. They may make some more or tweak again and test again – always in small batches. If a garment doesn't sell, it is disposed of rapidly.

▶

▶ The whole system relies on speed and agility in the supply chain. Each garment produced has a certain exclusivity about it, due to the small batch sizes, so can command a price premium – which more than covers the extra costs of Zara's highly responsive supply chain.

It is a highly successful model, honed over two decades, and one that no competitor has as yet come close to emulating. Established players would need to reinvent their whole supply chain.

Zara does not even advertise. To the envy, one presumes, of the likes of Benetton, with its United Colors shock-advertisement campaigns, it has never needed to.

Even in an industry as mature as fashion retailing, Zara shows that it is still possible to derive a business model with a sustainable competitive advantage.

As they might say in La Coruña, *viva la differencia*!

10

The product/market matrix (Ansoff)

This tool will help you:

- Clarify whether your growth strategy depends on existing or new products or existing or new markets
- Understand that new products or new markets incur incremental risk
- Beware the compounding of risk by aiming for new products into new markets (and even into new geographies)

About the tool

'When we're in a peak, we make a ton of money, and as soon as we make a ton of money, we're desperately looking for a way to spend it. And we diversify into areas that, frankly, we don't know how to run very well,' mused Bill Ford, great grandson of Henry.

Ford's story is not unique nor new. Igor Ansoff, author of the first book exclusively on corporate strategy in 1965, created his product/market matrix to illustrate the inherent risks of four generic growth strategies – growth through market penetration, market development, product development and diversification.

He argued that diversification, straying too far from what you know best, is by far the riskiest strategy. Ford might agree.

How to use it

Draw a 2 × 2 matrix, with existing and new products along the x-axis and existing and new markets along the y-axis – see Figure 10.1. Take your main sales initiatives planned for the next three to five years and place them in the relevant quadrant – along with their proportionate contribution to the overall forecast sales increase in that period.

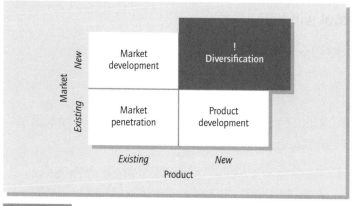

Figure 10.1 The product/market matrix

Source: Adapted from H. Igor Ansoff, 'Strategies for Diversification', *Harvard Business Review*, Sep-Oct 1957

Which quadrant shows the greatest uplift in sales? If it is in existing products to existing or new markets, or new products to existing markets, there should be no due cause for alarm. If it is the quadrant of new products to new markets, that is another story.

Ansoff's main intent was to stress that a diversification strategy, that of growth through launching new products into new markets, operated on a very much higher plane of risk than the other three strategies. Superficially attractive, and practised by many leading companies of his time, it is risky. While the first three strategies built on familiar skills in production, purchasing, sales and marketing, this was unlikely to be the case with diversification. Furthermore, diversification stood the risk of absorbing a disproportionately high proportion of managerial and engineering resources, due simply to the lack of familiarity with the new venture.

In later years, Ansoff came to believe that the matrix was an oversimplification, due to the different degrees of risk associated with new **market segment** entry and new **country market** entry. So he introduced the third dimension of new geography. Thus his two-dimensional 2 × 2 matrix became 3D, a 2 × 2 × 2 cube.

The extremes of risk were now even more highlighted. The greater the diversification, the greater the compounded risk. The risk of pursuing a strategy of a new product serving a new market segment in a new geographic market was of a very different order of magnitude from a strategy of further market penetration by an existing product in an existing market segment in an existing geographical market.

When to use it – or be wary

The Ansoff matrix helps to crystallise the riskiness of a proposed strategy. Whether the matrix itself is deployed, or merely the thinking underlying it, the manager should always be conscious of the compounding effect on risk from a growth strategy premised on new products **and** new markets **and** new geographies.

Ansoff's complete strategic planning model, however, was complex, overly so in the eyes of some critics. Ansoff himself came to be concerned that it might come to result in 'paralysis by analysis'.

But one component of his model, the product/market matrix, has stood the test of time. It is simple, self-evident and rams home an important message – beware of compounding each element of risk in a growth strategy.

case study

Using it: Virgin Cola

We saw previously, in the cases of Virgin Group (Tool 8) and Virgin Galactic (Tool 2), how each outpost of the Virgin empire benefits from the cachet of the Virgin brand – a brand that represents not only value for money and the little guy versus the big guy, but a brush of glamour.

But the magic touch doesn't always work. Virgin Cola was launched in 1994, with Richard Branson seeking to take on the 'global duopoly' of Coca-Cola and Pepsi. He demonstrated this with his customary reserve by driving a Sherman tank into Times Square, New York City, and crushing rivals' cola bottles beneath its tracks.

The venture ticked the box of giant-killing, but how was Branson to deliver value for money? He could come nowhere near to achieving the economies of scale, not only in production but in marketing, of the two powerhouses.

And how much excitement or glamour can you squeeze into a bottle of cola? A litre of cola in the supermarket is just a litre of cola, whether it carries the brand of the Big Two, the supermarket's own brand or a Virgin – to all but the Coke/Pepsi obsessives of this world.

It is not far off being a commodity, like a litre of milk, a litre of carbonated water, a kilo of butter. You can glamorise the marketing, but not the product.

Virgin Cola was finally closed in 2012. That hurt: 'I thought I could knock Coca-Cola into touch,' said Branson later, 'It didn't quite work out.'

The attractiveness/advantage matrix (GE/McKinsey)

This tool will help you:

- In business strategy, reveal your strategic position
- Decide whether to invest, hold onto or exit your business segments or enter new ones
- In corporate strategy, unveil the same findings for the strategic business units in your multi-business company

About this tool

Where should your business compete? In which segments? Why? How?

Answering those questions is your first step in targeting the strategic gap, optimising your business mix.

You need to undertake a portfolio analysis of your main business segments, and the best tool for this is the GE/McKinsey attractiveness/advantage matrix.

The matrix will show how competitive your firm is in segments ranked by order of market attractiveness. Ideally you should invest in segments where you are strongest and/or which are the most attractive. And you should consider withdrawal from segments where you are weaker and/or where your competitive position is untenable.

And, perhaps, should you be looking to enter another business segment (or segments) in **more** attractive markets than the ones you address currently? If so, do you have grounds for believing that you would be at least reasonably placed in this new segment? And that soon you could become well placed?

How to use it

First, you need to specify how to define an 'attractive' market segment. This is, to some extent, sector-specific, and no two strategists will come up with the same list, but over the years I have found these five factors to be both pertinent and relatively measurable:

1 **Market size** – relative to that of other segments

2 **Market demand growth** – perhaps derived from the HOOF approach of Tool 5

3 **Competitive intensity** – derived from the Five Forces model of Tool 6

4 **Industry profitability** – average operating margin compared to other segments

5 **Market risk** – cyclicality, volatility (for example, exposure to country risk).

The larger the market and the faster it is growing, the more attractive, other things being equal, is the market. Likewise, the greater the industry profitability. But be careful with the other two factors, where the converse applies. The **greater** the competitive intensity and the **greater** its risk, the **less** attractive is the market.

You could argue that taking even just these five factors is, effectively, double counting certain of them. Market demand growth is a major determinant of internal rivalry, itself one of the five forces in competitive intensity, which is the prime driver of industry profitability. Market risk may be inversely proportional to industry profitability.

Any list will be unscientific, but it should be instructive. You will have to use your own judgement on the composition of the factors, as well as their weighting. Easiest is to give each of the five an equal weighting, so a rating for overall market attractiveness would be the simple average of the ratings for each factor.

You may, however, be risk averse and attach a higher importance to the market risk factor. In this case, you would derive a weighted average.

An example may help – see Table 11.1. Suppose your business is in four product/market segments and you are contemplating entering a fifth. You rate each of the segments against each of the criteria for market attractiveness. Segment D emerges as the most attractive, followed by new segment E. B is rather unattractive. In assessing overall attractiveness, you have gone for a simple average of the ratings against each factor. You could instead have opted for a weighting system, yielding a weighted average. Or you could, say, have double counted one of the factors, say risk. More accurate, perhaps, but here you opted for simplicity.

Table 11.1 Market attractiveness: an example

Segments	A	B	C	D	E (new)
Market size	3	2	2	3	3
Market growth	1	2	3	5	5
Competitive intensity	2	2	3	4	5
Industry profitability	3	3	4	2	2
Market risk	5	2	4	4	2
Overall attractiveness	**2.8**	**2.2**	**3.2**	**3.6**	**3.4**

Key to rating: 1 = Unattractive, 3 = Reasonably attractive, 5 = Highly attractive
[For competitive intensity, remember that the more intense the competition, the *less* attractive the market. Likewise for market risk, the riskier the market, the *less* attractive it is]

Next you pull out the ratings of competitive position you undertook in Tool 7 for each segment. Now you can draw up the attractiveness/advantage chart, by placing each segment in the appropriate part of the matrix (see Figure 11.1). Segment A, for example, has a competitive position rating of 4.0 (out of 5) and a market attractiveness rating of 2.8 (also out of 5).

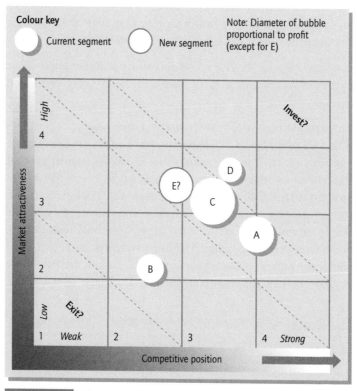

Figure 11.1   The attractiveness/advantage matrix: an example
Source: General Electric, McKinsey & Co. and various

The segment's position in the chart will reflect both its competitive position (along the x-axis) and its market attractiveness (along the y-axis). The size of each circle should be roughly proportional to the segment's contribution to operating profit.

The closer your segment is positioned towards the top right-hand corner, the better placed it is. Above the top right dotted diagonal, you should invest further in that segment, building on your advantage. Should the segment sink below the bottom left dotted diagonal, however, you should harvest the business for cash or consider withdrawal. Segments placed along the main diagonal are reasonably placed and should be held, with investment cases carefully scrutinised.

The overall strategic position shown in the example seems sound. It shows favourable strength in the biggest and reasonably attractive segment C, and an excellent position in the somewhat less attractive segment A. Segment D is highly promising and demands more attention, given the currently low level of profit.

Segment B should, perhaps, be exited – it's a rather unattractive segment, and your firm is not that well placed. The new segment E seems promising.

You may consider the following strategic options worthy of further analysis:

■ Holding and steady development in segments A and C

■ Investment in segment D

■ Entry to segment E (with competitive position improving over time as market share develops)

■ Harvesting or exit from segment B.

How is the overall strategic position in your business? Hopefully your **main** segments, from which you derive most revenues, should find themselves positioned above the main diagonal.

Do you have any new segments in mind? How attractive are they? How well placed would you be?

Are there any segments you should be thinking of getting out of?

Which segments are so important that you would derive greatest benefit from improving your competitive position? Where should you concentrate your efforts?

When to use it – or be wary

This tool is the essence of strategy, to be used on any strategy development process.

And yet a major criticism of this portfolio planning tool lies in its subjectivity. Some argue that there are so many subjective calls made throughout the process that deriving strategy from its findings is fraught with danger, thus:

- Factors to derive market attractiveness are chosen subjectively, as is their weighting
- Key success factors (KSFs) used to determine competitive position are derived partially from objectively sourced customer purchasing criteria, but the weighting between them and other KSFs, such as market share or management, involves judgement
- Rating your firm's capabilities against the KSFs to derive competitive position is laced with subjectivity and may be sprinkled with false pride – managers may be reticent to admit that they are weaker than key competitors against certain KSFs.

The counter argument to the final bullet is that managers who behave preciously over their fiefdoms are soon brought down to earth at strategy workshops.

The criticism of the tool's reliance on judgement is accepted but misplaced. Strategy is all about judgement, albeit backed up by fact where available. The process of constructing the attractiveness/advantage matrix is illuminating, instructive and crucial to strategy development. It forces you to think about what drives success in your business, how your business has fared to date against those capabilities and what you need to do about them in the future. It is not only a portfolio planning tool, but the first step in identifying the strategic gap.

You need to bear in mind, however, two caveats when using the tool. Neither invalidates it, but they merit recognition. They are:

- **Definition of the relevant market.** Your firm may be poorly placed in relation to the whole market, but well placed in a niche corner of that market. Lotus may have an infinitesimal share of the UK automobile market, but it has a significant share of the luxury end of the market and a good share of the luxury performance niche. Any decisions taken on the Lotus business, based on an attractiveness/advantage matrix relating to the whole UK automobile market, would be misleading.

■ **Inter-business synergies.** Your firm may be poorly placed in one business, but it may serve as a loss leader for a strong position in another, better placed business. This is especially the case when the matrix is used in business strategy, with some product/market segments persevered with only due to the potential loss of credibility in withdrawal affecting business in the core segments.

These limitations exist and need to be managed, again using judgement. No strategy tools can obviate the need for judgement. Nor should they be expected to.

Think of military strategy. Sure, there are tomes on classic strategies. But, when in the field, much will depend ultimately on judgement, often of one general or admiral. Nelson got it right at Trafalgar, Haig not so at the Somme – a gain of five miles in five months at an average loss of 5,000 men a day was a terrible indictment of one man's judgement. The strategic alternative, evident perhaps only in retrospect, of holding the line for as long as it took for technological advance (the tank) to enable breakthrough might have saved countless lives.

case study

Using it: Extramural Ltd

This tool is so important in both business and corporate strategy (Tool 16) that I shall summarise here a fictional case study, that of Extramural Ltd, a notionally leading player in the UK market for school activity and educational tours, which I develop in greater detail in another book, *The FT Essential Guide to Developing a Business Strategy: How to Use Strategic Planning to Start Up or Grow Your Business.*

▶

In their strategy development process, the owners draw up an attractiveness/ advantage matrix for their school activity tour business (see Figure 11.2).

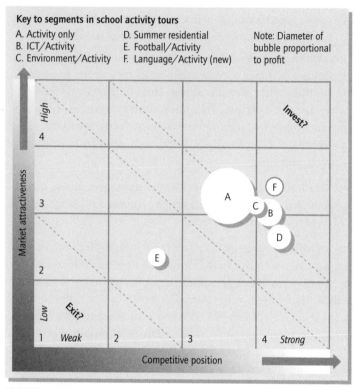

Key to segments in school activity tours

A. Activity only
B. ICT/Activity
C. Environment/Activity

D. Summer residential
E. Football/Activity
F. Language/Activity (new)

Note: Diameter of bubble proportional to profit

Figure 11.2 Extramural Ltd: strategic position in school activity tours

This shows immediately that Extramural's strategic position here is sound – it has favourable to strong positions in segments that are, in the main, attractive.

The new language/activity tour segment (F) seems the most promising, with summer residential camps (D) less so, despite faster growth, due to relatively low occupancy and profitability.

The exception is football/activity tours (E). Dominated by one long-established specialist player, Footie4Kids, Extramural's position is tenable but the market the least attractive of all.

Unless they can find strong links and synergies with other segments, the owners may need to consider withdrawal from this segment.

They embark on a gap analysis exercise – profiling the ideal player, identifying the strategic gap and targeting how they should bridge it.

They conclude that they should strive to enhance the business's generic strategy of differentiation, but with some repositioning in key segments. They set their sights on these targets (see Figure 11.3):

■ Strengthen competitive position in pure activity tours through addressing shortcomings identified in a customer survey

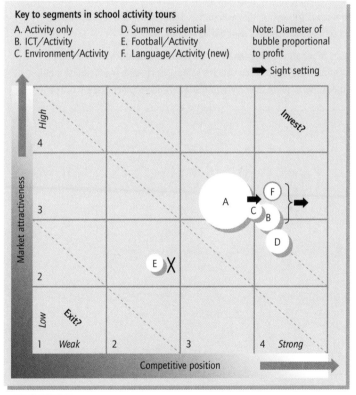

Key to segments in school activity tours

A. Activity only   D. Summer residential   Note: Diameter of
B. ICT/Activity   E. Football/Activity   bubble proportional
C. Environment/Activity   F. Language/Activity (new)   to profit

➡ Sight setting

Figure 11.3 Extramural Ltd: target strategic position in school activity tours

- Boost competitive position in combined learning/activity tours through a strategy of differentiation – using the forthcoming, budgeted campaign to roll out the language/activity product as a springboard for repositioning
- Withdraw from football/activity tours, a segment that makes little contribution once marketing costs are fully attributed.

The owners proceed to develop more specific profit growth initiatives in each of the segments to be retained. They insert a new column into their competitive position rating table (Tool 7) to represent Extramural in three years' time and adjust the ratings to reflect the target impact of the new business strategy. Then they add a further column to anticipate the competitive response of the market leader to Extramural's strategic initiatives.

If the strategy is successful, they will narrow that differential with the market leader in school activity tours over the next three years.

The owners move on to similar analyses for their other businesses (day camps and educational tours) and then use this same attractiveness/advantage matrix tool as the cornerstone of their corporate strategy development (see Tool 16).

12

The growth/share matrix (BCG)

This tool will help you:

- Set out the relative strategic positioning of each major segment (or business, in corporate strategy)
- Pinpoint areas for investment, holding or withdrawal
- Provide more quantification, less subjectivity than that of Tool 11

About this tool

'If you want a friend, get a dog,' pronounced corporate raider Carl Icahn. He meant that you don't expect to make friends in his line of business, not that you should go out and buy a dog business.

The latter, as defined by The Boston Consulting Group (BCG), is one where you have a low relative market share in a slow-growing market. The growth/share matrix, along with its catchy menagerie, is one of those tools that has held firm over time. It first appeared in the late 1960s and is as widely used today as ever.

Its aims are, essentially, the same as those of the attractiveness/advantage matrix (Tool 11), charting the relative position of the entities analysed – whether product/market segments within one business unit or business units within a multi-business company.

Where it differs is in its choice of parameters:

■ Instead of a somewhat subjective assessment of **market attractiveness**, it opts for one measurable parameter, **market demand growth**

■ Instead of a somewhat subjective assessment of **competitive position**, it opts for one measurable parameter, **relative market share**.

The growth/share matrix offers, in essence, an objective, measurable proxy for the attractiveness/advantage matrix.

How to use it

Draw up a 2 × 2 matrix, with these axes:

■ **Relative market share (RMS) along the x-axis** – not market share in itself, but your market share relative to that of your leading competitor. Market share on its own is no indicator of relative strength; having a market share of 20 per cent may be a strength in a highly fragmented market where your nearest competitor has 10 per cent and other main competitors are in single figures, but that 20 per cent takes on a different complexion if you are in a concentrated market where the leader has 40 per cent; in the first market, your relative market share would be 2.0×, but in the second 0.5× – implying very different prospects for sustaining competitive advantage.

■ **Market growth along the y-axis** – taken as the forecast annual average growth rate in real terms over the next three to five years.

Plot your product/market segments (or businesses, in corporate strategy) accordingly and reveal the following:

■ **The 'stars'**: those segments that are in the top right quadrant, where you have high share in a fast-growing market

■ **The 'cash cows'**: those in the bottom right segment, where you have high share in a slow-growing market

⬛ **The 'question marks'**: those in the top left quadrant, where you have low share in a fast-growing market

⬛ **The 'dogs'**: those in the bottom left quadrant, where you have low share in a slow-growing market.

Other things being equal, you should invest in your stars, harvest your cash cows, divest your dogs and analyse carefully the risks and returns of investing in your question marks.

In Figure 12.1, the example used in Tool 11 is revisited. The segment circles are left in exactly the same positions as they were in Figure 11.1. This is a simplifying assumption and is unlikely to be the case in practice. A market attractiveness ranking may not be

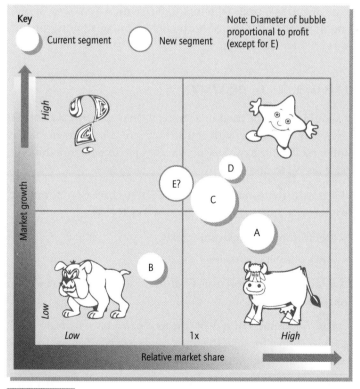

Figure 12.1   **The growth/share matrix: an example**

Source: Adapted from The Boston Consulting Group (www.bcg.com)

the same as that for market growth. Likewise, for relative market share and competitive position – see below under 'When to use it – or be wary'.

Again, you may consider the following strategic options worthy of further analysis:

- Milking of cash cow A
- Holding and possible investment in borderline cash cow/star C
- Investment in definitive star D
- Likely entry to borderline question mark/star E
- Harvesting or exit from dog B.

How is the portfolio of segments in your business? Hopefully your main segments, from which you derive most revenues, should find themselves positioned in the right-hand quadrants, the cash cows and stars. Any dogs?

When to use it – or be wary

It should always be used in a strategy development process, but preferably in parallel with the attractiveness/advantage matrix. If the results of the two matrices show up contradictory findings, delve deeper to find out why.

The growth/share matrix shares some of the caveats of the attractiveness/advantage matrix, as discussed in Tool 11:

- Definition of the relevant market
- Inter-business synergies.

Be aware of these limitations but don't let them stop you from using the tool.

A more important critique of this tool stems from its main claim to fame. Unlike those of the attractiveness/advantage matrix, the axes show single, objective, measurable parameters.

Proponents of the growth/share matrix argue that these parameters are genuinely indicative of the parameters of the attractiveness/advantage matrix:

▪ Relative market share has been shown in many studies to be correlated with profit, hence competitive position, due to economies of scale on the cost side and perhaps to premium pricing on the revenue side

▪ Market demand growth is indicative of market attractiveness because there is greater opportunity to gain share in a market where all are growing than in a market that is stagnant and where players are fighting to maintain share.

Opponents, however, believe the parameters on the growth/share matrix represent an over-simplification:

▪ Relative market share can be an indicator of competitive advantage, but it may not be; equally important is market share change. History is full of examples of companies with formerly high market shares that have since tumbled to earth, and of the converse – companies with little share storming a market. Think of the examples of IBM, which fell, and Dell, which rose, in the personal computer market – IBM's relative market share in the early days proved of little competitive advantage against its more nimble rivals. Use of the growth/share matrix in the 1970s might have misled IBM, whereas use of the attractiveness/advantage matrix might have pinpointed shortfalls in cost base, product development and distribution.

▪ Market growth is an equally crude indicator of market attractiveness – again, it may be indicative of relevant industry profitability, or it may not be. Unlike in the attractiveness/advantage matrix, it ignores the supply side; the market may be growing fast, but, if there is an overdose of suppliers, competition will be intense and the market will not be attractive.

Again, though, these limitations should not stop you using the tool. Be conscious of its shortcomings and use it alongside the attractiveness/advantage matrix. Together, they invariably produce useful insights.

case study

Using it: Extramural Ltd

The growth/share matrix is used often in business strategy, but is demonstrated more clearly when applied in corporate strategy – see Tool 16 and Figure 16.3 for its use on Extramural Ltd.

Three generic strategies (Porter)

This tool will help you:

- Determine which generic strategy you should pursue
- Clarify subsequent strategic and tactical investment decisions
- Ensure you are not a middle-of-the-road player, in danger of being run over

About this tool

Clowns to the left, jokers to the right, Stealers Wheel in the early 1970s were 'stuck in the middle...'. Not the place to be in business either, according to Michael Porter.

This is another area of business strategy where Porter's mastery of the synthesis of industry economics has been influential and long-lasting. As with his Five Forces in industry analysis (Tool 6) and his value chain (Tool 9), his three generic strategies have been with us since the early 1980s and still form the base camp whence strategists ascend to the peak.

His three generic business-level strategies are:

- Cost leadership
- Differentiation
- Focus.

Any one of these strategies can give sustainable competitive advantage. Pursue two or all three of these strategies in the same business and you will, in all probability, end up 'stuck in the middle' – a recipe for long-term under-performance.

How to use it

What is the primary source of competitive advantage in your business? Is it cost? Or is it the distinctiveness of your product and/or service offering?

Think back to Tool 7, where you rated your business in its key product/market segments against its key success factors (KSFs). Did your business get higher ratings against the cost KSFs or the differentiation KSFs?

And go back one stage further. Did you give a higher weighting to differentiation factors than to cost factors? Or the other way round?

There is little to be gained in being a cost leader in a segment that is not price sensitive. Likewise, in being a highly differentiated producer in a segment where customers perceive little differentiation.

If cost factors are most important in your business and you rated well, or at least promisingly, against them, then you should opt for a strategy of cost leadership.

If differentiating factors are more important and you rated well, or at least promisingly, against them, you should pursue a strategy of differentiation.

Either strategy can yield a sustainable competitive advantage. Either you supply a product that is at a lower cost than competitors' products or you supply a product that is sufficiently differentiated from competitors that customers are prepared to pay a premium price – where the incremental price charged adequately covers the incremental costs of supplying the differentiated product.

For a ready example of a successful low-cost strategy, think of easyJet or Ryanair, where relentless maximisation of load factor enables them to offer seats at scarcely credible prices compared with those that prevailed before they entered the scene, and still produce a profit. Or think of IKEA stylish, but highly price-competitive, furniture.

A classic example of the differentiation strategy would be Apple. Never the cheapest, whether in PCs, laptops or mobile phones, but always stylistically distinctive and feature-intensive. Or Pret A Manger in fresh, high-quality fast food.

These two strategies were well recognised before Porter introduced his generic strategies. He identified a third, the focus strategy (see Figure 13.1). While acknowledging that a firm typically can prosper in its industry by following either a low-cost or differentiation strategy, one alternative is to not address the whole industry but narrow the scope and focus on a slice of it, a single segment.

Under these circumstances, a firm can achieve market leadership through focus and differentiation leading over time to scale and experience-driven low unit costs (see Tool 14) compared to less focused players in that segment.

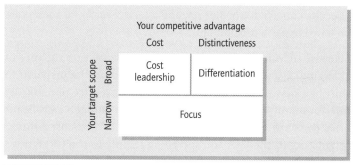

Figure 13.1   **Three generic strategies**   Source: Adapted from Michael E. Porter, *Competitive Strategy*, Free Press, 1980

The classic example of a successful focus strategy is Honda motorcycles, whose focus on product reliability over decades yielded the global scale to enable its differentiated, quality products to remain cost competitive.

When to use it – or be wary

When drawing up a strategy, you must be absolutely clear which generic strategy you are following. You do not want to be stuck in the middle.

If you find you are more differentiated than some players, but less than others, and higher cost than some players, but lower cost than others, you are a middle-of-the-road player. This is unsafe territory.

Beware, too, of change. Any generic strategy is vulnerable to shifting customer needs and preferences. No strategy should be set in stone.

If you pursue a low-cost strategy, beware of a shift in customer needs putting a greater emphasis on quality, for which customers are prepared to pay a higher price. An example is the cinema industry. For years many chains followed a policy of shoving the customers into their 'flea pits', keeping costs down to a minimum. Customers deserted in droves, opting for the comfort of their living rooms and the ease of the video recorder. Today some cinemas offer reclining seats and waiter service – the diametrically opposite concept to the flea pit, and a service many customers are prepared to pay a premium for.

Likewise, if you pursue a strategy of differentiation, beware of changing customer preferences. Customers may be prepared to shift to a new entrant offering a product or service of markedly inferior quality to yours, but good enough and at a significant price discount. The classic example is that of low-cost airlines, originating in the USA and spreading rapidly to the UK, Europe and Asia, and forcing the full service national carriers to radically rethink their business model.

The canny business will spot the emergent trend and open a new business, preferably under a new brand, so as not to blur the image of the brand in the eyes of the customer. They will pursue one generic strategy in one business and a different one in another.

There is, however, no guarantee of success in the new business, given that it will operate in an entirely different culture – for example the short-lived airline Go, launched by British Airways to address the booming low-cost market and eventually swallowed by easyJet. Likewise, attempts by Ford Motor Company to move into more differentiated businesses via acquisition proved not to be value enhancing and the Jaguar and Land Rover divisions were soon resold.

But it is especially inadvisable to mix strategies in one business, even if you are doing so in different segments. By definition, a strategic business unit operates in product/market segments that are inter-related – whether by offering the same or similar products or services or addressing the same or similar customer groups. One strategy in one segment coupled with another strategy in another segment can not only confuse the customer but again land you 'stuck in the middle'.

Finally, Jules Goddard, in an award-winning 2013 article, challenges the 'fatal bias' of companies towards cost cutting and attempting to pursue a low-cost strategy. He builds on the work of Michael Raynor and Mumtaz Ahmed, where, in a huge study of 25,000 companies, only a handful were found to have driven sustained superior financial performance through following a low-cost strategy.

Goddard believes that companies should rather pursue a policy of strategic innovation, constantly probing new areas in the way pharmaceutical companies carry out clinical trials. He suggests business planning should focus only on ideas, not on numbers.

And, intriguingly, he teases that managers should be tasked with the complete reversal of their usual challenge. Instead of being asked to take 10 per cent off their cost base, they should be set challenges such as this: 'If we were required to carry a 20 per cent premium price on our products and services, how would we change our thinking?'

Goddard's article, along with his 2011 book *Uncommon Sense, Common Nonsense*, co-authored with Tony Eccles, is as stimulating and provocative a read as is to be found anywhere in contemporary management thinking.

---

case study

Using it: Southwest Airlines

The Southwest story is well known, but remains the quintessential example of Porter's generic low-cost strategy. It is one of the elite companies in history that have turned an industry's rules of the game upside down, not just in the USA, but throughout the world.

What Southwest strived to do from the outset is what it has consistently and profitably achieved. Its goal was 'to meet customers' short-haul travel needs at fares competitive with the cost of automobile travel'.

A low-cost strategy both requires and creates high utilisation – in the case of airlines, this is measured as load factor – the proportion of paid-for seats on the average flight. From the start, Southwest packed in the passengers – primarily through offering extraordinary fares, like the renowned 'Pleasure Class' $13 from Dallas to Houston, but also through engendering a sense of fun (and 'luv') on board, like stewardesses hanging out of overhead lockers.

But that was just the top line. To turn a profit, Southwest also had to keep costs as low as conceivable at every stage of the value chain, including:

- Point-to-point flights – no use of hub and spoke services, thereby speeding up turnaround times and maximising average flying hours per day, and improving punctuality

- New aircraft – minimising downtime and improving punctuality again

- A single type of aircraft, the Boeing 737, thereby minimising costs of spares, storage, mechanic and pilot training, repairs and maintenance, and achieving purchasing economies

- Use of secondary city airports, like Chicago Midway
- No frills – no seat allocation, with no boarding preference for frequent fliers or higher fare passengers (until recently), basic, standard, single-class seating and no meals (just refreshments purchasable on board), thereby facilitating intra-flight cleaning and speeding up flight turnaround times
- Non-traditional union representation, with specific Southwest unions for pilots and flight attendants formed to represent their interests
- From the late 1990s, most booking and checking-in done over the Web
- A lean, well compensated management structure
- Careful hedging of fuel prices.

From its origins as an intra-state Texan airbus operator, Southwest became not just the most highly capitalised airline in the USA but also a role model to budget carriers throughout the Americas, Europe and Asia – from JetBlue to easyJet, Azul Brasilian to Air Asia.

'You are now free to move about the country' was an early tagline of the airline. They were unduly modest. For 'country', read 'world'.

14

The experience curve (BCG)

This tool will help you:

■ Confirm that experience effects are an economic fact of life

■ Pursue a strategic advantage if your firm has greater experience

■ Be alerted to the risk of your experience being shared by competitors

About this tool

Albert Einstein said that 'the only source of knowledge is experience'. So, too, with cost competitiveness.

In the previous tool, a focus strategy was shown to combine elements of both the differentiation and low-cost strategies. This was due largely to the effects of the experience curve.

A 'learning curve' effect had long been recognised in industry before The Boston Consulting Group got in on the act. Managers understood that the more often a manufacturing task was performed, the less labour time it took to complete the next similar task. Initial quantification at a US airforce base in the 1920s suggested that each doubling of cumulative production of First

World War aeroplanes led to a decrease in the total labour time to build one unit of 10–15 per cent.

Forty years on, BCG transformed this thinking. In a series of studies on a broad range of industries, from beer and toilet paper to machinery and industrial components, they found that a similar relationship existed across the board. Their 'law of experience' found that 'the unit cost of value added to a standard product declines by a constant percentage (typically between 20 and 30 per cent) each time cumulative output doubles' – see Figure 14.1.

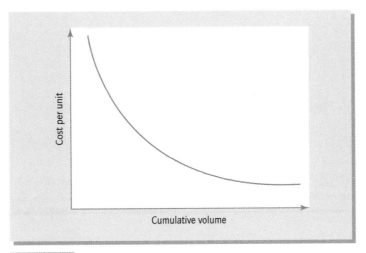

Figure 14.1 **The experience curve**   Source: Adapted from The Boston Consulting Group (www.bcg.com)

BCG ascribed to their law of experience a series of causes, in particular:

▪ Labour efficiency – workers learn the tricks of the trade, what works, what doesn't, what shortcuts to take – and managers, too

▪ Process efficiency – processes become optimized and more standardised

▪ Technology efficiency – process automation displaces labour inputs.

BCG's research was broad and comprehensive, but not new. Where they broke new ground came in their interpretation of the research and its implications for strategy. If the player with the largest cumulative experience would have the lowest unit costs of production, then strategy should be aimed at maximising sales and production, hence market share, rather than maximising profit.

This was the theoretical underpinning of BCG's growth/share matrix (see Tool 12). Due to the experience curve, relative market share should be a firm indicator of relative cost position. Indeed BCG created a table setting out a typical relationship (see Figure 14.2).

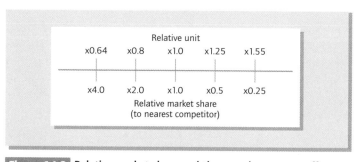

Figure 14.2 Relative market share and the experience curve effect: an example

Source: Adapted from Bruce Henderson, *The Experience Curve Reviewed*, The Boston Consulting Group, 1973 (reprint No 135)

How to use it

Building on your analysis in Tool 13, consider a strategic option whereby you invest heavily in market share gain in a segment where you already have a high market share – and are preferably the market leader.

By gaining further market share, to what extent will the experience curve effect enable you to further reduce unit costs? If this were to be translated into reduced pricing rather than increased margin, what effect would that have on your competitors?

Would they retaliate? Could they? Could your strategy force some of the weakest competitors to withdraw from the segment?

When to use it – or be wary

You should always take into account the experience curve in drawing up your strategic options.

Bruce Henderson was aware of its main strategic limitation, namely shared experience in the industry. Referring to Figure 14.2, he wrote: 'Characteristically, a normal experience curve slope will produce cost ratios to the largest competitor like these; where the cost differential is less than this, it is usually because of shared experience... [or] by inadequate investment or poor management.'

Shared experience between competitors can come about in a number of ways – through papers, seminars, conferences, supplier briefings but, perhaps most of all, through consulting promiscuity and labour mobility. If you know that your competitor has developed a better production process, you would be wise to either engage the same consulting group that advised your competitor or recruit one or two of their former employees.

Also, even if your unit costs are lower because your relative market share is high, such factors remain only part of the story. Differentiation factors may prove critical. If a competitor comes to market with a product that is technologically superior, your lower unit costs on your technologically inferior product will be of little comfort as customers switch to the new product.

case study

Using it: New energy technologies

Much academic research has been conducted on the experience curve. While no one yet has found a theoretical explanation for its quantification, numerous empirical studies have been undertaken, confirming it as a correlation phenomenon, as opposed to an established theory.

One such is fascinating in our energy-conscious, warming globe. A 2006 study into new energy technologies by Lund University in

▶ Sweden found that the unit cost of each technology is falling in a manner that matches the experience curve – with one exception: nuclear energy.

In this research, a 'progress ratio' is defined as one minus the percentage decrease in unit costs of production following a doubling of cumulative production. Thus a progress ratio of 80 per cent implies that the unit cost of the product decreases by 20 per cent with each doubling in cumulative production.

They found that progress ratios ranged from around 80 per cent for technologies such as photovoltaics, wind turbines and fuel cells, 85–90 per cent for biomass (wood chips) and solar thermal and 90–100 per cent for advanced fossil-fuel technologies (coal, gas, oil, CO_2 capture). Nuclear they placed in the range 95–105 per cent, implying a possible reverse experience curve.

In other words, and in short, the unit costs, in terms of euros/kilowatt-hour, of alternative energy technologies are on the way down, thanks to the experience curve.

There is hope yet for the planet.

Blue ocean strategy
(Kim and Mauborgne)

This tool will help you:

- Seek an alternative to slugging it out, face to face, fist to fist with your competitors – and instead dodge them
- Reinvent the rules of the game by shifting the accepted norm of which factors are key to success
- Follow both a differentiation strategy and a low-cost strategy by creating your own 'value innovation'

About this tool

What if Porter is wrong?

One of the criticisms long aimed at Michael Porter's Five Forces industry analysis (Tool 6) is that it is too confined, too narrow in focus. The delineation of industry boundaries for analysis of the Five Forces and the shaping of a competitive strategy within that industry may constrict the strategist so rigidly that the opportunity for genuine value innovation **beyond current industry boundaries** may be lost.

Two academics from INSEAD, Chan Kim and Renee Mauborgne, argue that competing head-on in today's overcrowded industries results in nothing but a 'bloody red ocean of rivals fighting over a shrinking profit pool'. Based on a study of 150 strategic moves over a 100-year period they argue that tomorrow's winners will succeed not by battling in red oceans but by creating 'blue oceans of uncontested market space ripe for growth'.

In a red ocean you fight competitors tooth and nail in an existing market space. In a blue ocean you swim jauntily in an uncontested market space – new demand is created and competitors become irrelevant.

Such strategic moves create genuine 'value innovation', or 'powerful leaps in value for both firm and buyers, rendering rivals obsolete'.

They quote examples such as Apple's iTunes and Cirque du Soleil. Apple created a new market space by teaming up with the music companies to offer legal online music downloading, thereby consigning pioneer Napster (bane of the music companies) to history. Cirque du Soleil reinvented the circus industry by blending it with ballet to create a new market space.

They argue further that the conventional choice of generic strategy between differentiation and low cost is also sub-optimal. That is the traditional choice faced by competitors in a red ocean. Blue ocean strategy enables the firm to do both, offering a differentiated product to a new market space at a cost sufficiently low to deter further entrants.

The holy grail of blue ocean strategy is to create:
Differentiated Product + Low Cost = Value Innovation.

They put forward six principles for creating and capturing blue oceans:

1   Reconstruct market boundaries
2   Focus on the big picture
3   Reach beyond existing demand

4 Get the strategic sequence right

5 Overcome organisational hurdles

6 Build execution into strategy.

They have developed a framework supported by a range of tools to put these principles into effect – see **www.blueoceanstrategy. com**. Two in particular will be elaborated on below.

How to use it

Kim and Mauborgne's Pioneer-Migrator-Settler map is a stimulating start point. Try plotting your portfolio of addressed product/ market segments on a matrix, as in Figure 15.1.

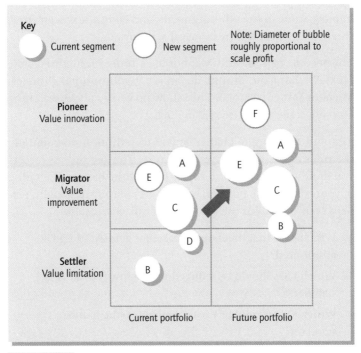

Figure 15.1 The Pioneer-Migrator-Settler map

Source: Adapted from W. Chan Kim and Renée Mauborgne, *Blue Ocean Strategy: How to Create Uncontested Market Space and Make the Competition Irrelevant*, Harvard Business School Press, 2005

Settler segments are those where you are a me-too player, migrators are where your competitive position is strong and pioneers are where you offer distinctive value.

If your current portfolio consists mainly of settlers, you are playing in a red ocean with dim prospects for sustainable, profitable growth. In your planned portfolio, you need to push into migratory or, best, pioneer segments.

If your current portfolio consists of settlers and migrators, your growth prospects may be reasonable but you are at risk of losing out to a pioneer competitor.

In the example shown, the firm is reasonably placed, with mainly migratory segments and just a couple of settlers. For the future, the firm is planning to exit segment B, differentiate further and improve value in the other segments, and enter a new segment F, where they will be a pioneering value innovator.

The second of Kim and Mauborgne's tools highlighted here tackles what you should do about a sub-optimal Pioneer-Migrator-Settler portfolio. They show how to go about searching for pioneer segments – see Figure 15.2.

Kim and Mauborgne challenge you to rethink fundamentally the rules of the game in your industry. The key success factors you drew up in Tool 7, and which formed the basis of the rating of your competitive position, need to be radically rethought, perhaps even, and this is their first port of call, eliminated:

- Which KSFs that the industry takes for granted should be **eliminated**?
- Which KSFs should be **reduced well below** the industry's standard?
- Which KSFs should be **raised well above** the industry's standard?
- Which KSFs that the industry has never offered should be **created**?

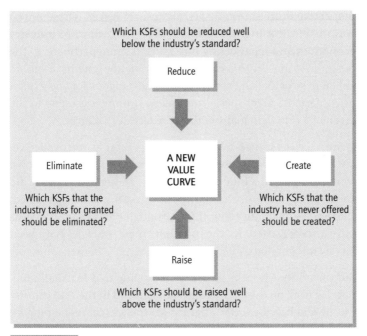

Figure 15.2   Rethinking key success factors for value innovation

Source: Adapted from W. Chan Kim and Renée Mauborgne, *Blue Ocean Strategy: How to Create Uncontested Market Space and Make the Competition Irrelevant*, Harvard Business School Press, 2005

In short, how can these KSFs be revised so that a new value curve is created, one that breaks the trade-off between differentiation and low-cost strategies?

When to use it – or be wary

Use blue ocean strategy when your red ocean strategy seems set to lead to unexciting growth prospects.

Kim and Mauborgne's work has received much criticism, some of it ill-founded and perhaps not unrelated to the phenomenal success of their book. Some say that there is little that is original in their work, with the concept of seeking uncontested market space little different from that, say, of Gary Hamel and C. K. Prahalad in *Competing for the Future* and their 'competing for industry foresight' (see Tool 19).

But similar criticism was levied at Michael Porter, whose genius was in synthesising the former ivory tower world of industry economics and repackaging it to make it more pertinent to the business world. In this case, Kim and Mauborgne have built a coherent structure and toolkit around how to look for and exploit uncontested market space – and made it more accessible to the business world than many of their predecessors' efforts.

Others criticise the model for being largely retrospective. Successful companies are, with the benefit of hindsight, shown to have deployed a blue ocean strategy, though when they did so they may have been unaware that such a strategy existed. Kim and Mauborgne admit this: 'Although blue ocean strategists have always existed, for the most part their strategies have been largely unconscious.'

But the critique is misplaced. It is like saying that Marshall's pioneering work on the price elasticity of demand in the 19th century was invalid because it was what market traders had been doing for centuries – chopping the price of an apple towards closing time, less so on a loaf of bread. Post-Marshall, business strategists were wiser. They adjusted prices, aware of likely elasticities. Likewise in the post-Kim and Mauborgne era: we can search for blue ocean strategy through changing the KSF rules of the game.

A more significant criticism concerns the usefulness of the model for the average business, whether small, medium or large. Nine times out of ten, strategy development will be about improving strategic position in red ocean markets. Blue ocean markets may exist, but they are riskier – often greatly riskier. For every Apple iTunes and Cirque du Soleil, there are scores of attempted blue ocean strategies that have foundered.

As Ansoff highlighted in the 1960s (see Tool 10), new products to new markets carry a degree of risk orders of a magnitude higher than new products to existing markets or existing products to new markets. iTunes was a new product to the new market, for Apple, of online downloading. It worked. Many such don't.

Risk, however, is no argument for debunking Kim and Mauborgne. It is an argument for embracing their blue ocean thinking and subjecting it to the rigours of risk analysis, for example in Tool 25, the Suns & Clouds Chart.

case study

Using it: Cirque du Soleil

Baie-Saint-Paul is a village nestling on the northern shores of the St Lawrence river in Quebec and it was there in the early 1980s that a small theatre troupe performed in the streets, entertaining residents and tourists with their stilt-walking, juggling, dancing, fire-breathing and music playing.

One such fire-breather was Guy Laliberté and, in 1984, he convinced the local authorities to let him take the popular act on a tour of the province. The Cirque du Soleil hasn't stopped touring since.

It never attempted to take head-on the might of Ringling Bros and the other circus groups. It would have had no chance competing in such a 'red ocean', where market demand was in steady decline, with customers lured elsewhere by competing forms of entertainment – movies, concerts, sports and television as before, but now too video games – and where costs, of both animal care and performers, were rising.

The Cirque opted for a blue ocean. It did not redefine the circus so much as invent a new art form, circus-cum-theatre-cum-dance-cum-spectacle.

Animals were out, sawdust too, while music, theatre and dance were in. Clowns stayed, but not slapstick. Acrobats were redisplayed in an elegant, arty setting. Shows were lent a theatrical theme and shows with different themes and content were performed from the same venue.

Revenues per square foot soared, not least because the shows were aimed not just at children, the mainstay of the old circus audience, but adults, too.

And costs were slashed – the large expense of feeding, training and caring for circus animals had been axed altogether.

The Cirque du Soleil pursued a strategy of differentiation – **and** it was lower cost. It has sailed in a sunny blue ocean to this day.

Optimising the corporate portfolio

These tools will help you:

- Optimise your portfolio of businesses from a helicopter perspective
- Decide which businesses you should invest in, which you should hang on to and monitor, which you should enter and which you should exit
- Gain a strategic framework for your allocation of corporate resources

About these tools

In the early 1980s, the new CEO of General Electric, Jack Welch, asked management guru Peter Drucker for advice. The latter responded with two questions that arguably changed the course of Welch's tenure: 'If you weren't already in a business, would you enter it today? And if the answer is no, what are you going to do about it?'

This led directly to a corporate strategy whereby every one of GE's businesses had to be either No. 1 or No. 2 in its sphere. If not, it would be fixed, sold or shut. The strategy worked.

Corporate strategy is not necessarily that different from business strategy. Often it can be just a timing or definitional issue

– a business unit of today may be a stand-alone corporation when sold to management tomorrow.

Nevertheless, corporate strategy tools are designed to address different questions. Whereas business strategy sets out to ask how a business can obtain a sustainable competitive advantage, corporate strategy asks three questions:

1   Which businesses should you be investing in?
2   Which businesses should you be acquiring or divesting?
3   Which resources common to all businesses should you focus on?

The second question will be looked at in the next tool on creating value in mergers, acquisitions and alliances. The third, on the resource-based view of strategy, will be discussed in Tool 19 on core competences. Here the focus is on knowing in which businesses you should be allocating your scarce resources.

You have already met the tools to do just that. You used them to determine the optimal balance of product/market segments within a business. Now you can use these very same tools to determine the optimal balance of businesses within a corporation.

These are they (as redisplayed in Figure 16.1):

- The attractiveness/advantage matrix (GE/McKinsey) – see Tool 11
- The growth/share matrix (BCG) – Tool 12.

These tools should give you a clear picture on which businesses you should:

- invest in
- hold and improve performance in
- exit
- enter.

How to use them

You should use these tools as set out in Tools 11 and 12, substituting the word 'business' for 'segment' all the way through.

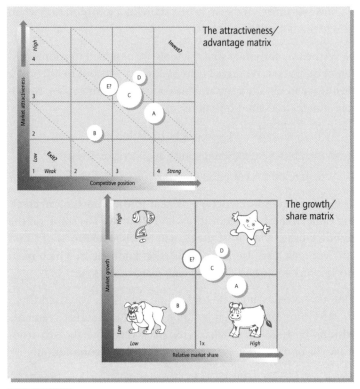

Figure 16.1 Corporate portfolio planning tools   Source: Tools 11 and 12

But there is one aspect that differs in corporate strategy – the option of buying and selling businesses. Specific tools for mergers, acquisitions and alliances (M&A) are set out in the next tool, but here it is useful to review the corporate strategic rationale behind M&A activity.

There are three main types of M&A strategy:

1   **Horizontal integration** – where you link up with a fellow producer, whether a direct or indirect competitor, to improve your collective competitive position

2   **Vertical integration** – where you link up with an operator further up the value chain (a customer) or further down (a supplier), to give you greater control of the market

3 **Diversification** – where you link up with a player in a different market altogether, but hopefully where there is sufficient compatibility between the two of you for synergistic benefits.

Horizontal integration is the most common M&A option. Vertical integration works for some (e.g. mobile phone operators setting up as retailers), not for others (e.g. kitchen furniture giant, Magnet, which ventured almost fatally into the high street in the late 1980s). Diversification was a fad of the 1970s and 1980s, with the likes of Hanson and Tomkins, but was proven to be a short-lived strategy, found to be dependent on taking over firms with sub-par financial planning systems.

Each of the above options has a converse. That of acquisition is divestment, which may well be a viable option – your unwanted business may find a home in another corporation where it is more wanted and so worthy of a reasonable exit price.

Likewise, vertical de-integration is common today – not just the selling off of businesses at different parts of the value chain, but the outsourcing of business processes.

When to use them – or be wary

If yours is a multi-business company, you would be advised to deploy these tools in every corporate strategy exercise.

The relative merits of the two main portfolio planning tools have already been set out in Tools 11 and 12. Take your pick. Me? I use them both. I like to spot the difference, if any, in the conclusions to be drawn from each tool – and then work out why.

But remember that the value of these matrices is only as good as the data and analysis put in. Your assessment of market attractiveness and competitive position in the attractiveness/advantage matrix must be rigorous and dispassionate. Your data on market growth and share in the growth/share matrix must be well researched – and relate to the right, specific markets.

There is a very old adage in management information systems: garbage in, garbage out. This applies with equal validity to portfolio planning tools.

case study

Using it: Extramural Ltd

The owners of Extramural Ltd have developed what they believe firmly to be a winning strategy for their school activity tours business – see Tool 11. They do the same for their two other businesses, educational tours and day camps, and draw up a strategic position chart for the company as a whole. They use the same GE/McKinsey chart as used in Tool 11, but this time the bubbles are for whole businesses, not segments within a business.

Extramural's strategic position seems clear at first glance (see Figure 16.2). The school activity tour business is well placed, with room for improvement, while the day-camp business may have promise – a tenable competitive position in an attractive market. But the educational tours business doesn't look good – a tenable competitive position in a relatively less attractive market.

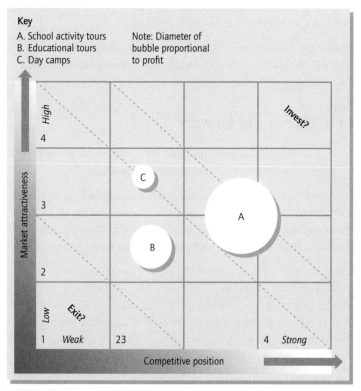

Key

A. School activity tours
B. Educational tours
C. Day camps

Note: Diameter of bubble proportional to profit

Figure 16.2 Extramural Ltd: strategic position

The owners feel they may already know the answer, but, to be sure, they seek a second opinion. They look to the BCG growth/share matrix (Tool 12) and plot the three businesses on that (see Figure 16.3).

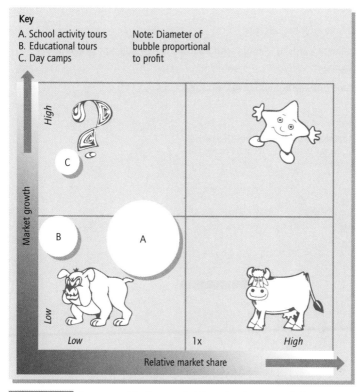

Key

A. School activity tours
B. Educational tours
C. Day camps

Note: Diameter of bubble proportional to profit

Market growth

High

Low

Low   1x   High

Relative market share

Figure 16.3 **Extramural Ltd: growth/share business portfolio**

Source: Adapted from The Boston Consulting Group (www.bcg.com)

None of the three businesses looks particularly happy here. At a market share relative to the leader (ActivTours) of 0.68 and operating in a slow growing market, even the school activity tours business comes out as a dog – though nowhere near as canine as the educational tours business, with a market share of 0.15 relative to the leader (STL) and a similarly lethargic market.

Day camps, however, is a question mark. Despite Extramural's late entry into the market and a mere 0.20 market share relative to the leader (Ultra Camps), it is a business operating in a fast-growing market, thus escaping the nomenclature of dog.

The corporate strategy the owners should pursue now stands out starkly (see Figure 16.4):

- Exit from educational tours
- Use the proceeds to invest in school activity tours, nudging that business from dog to cash cow. . .
- . . . and grow by acquisition in day camps.

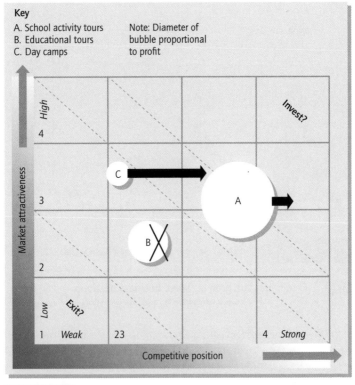

Figure 16.4   **Extramural Ltd: strategic repositioning**

But there is one further check the owners must do before they contemplate implementing this corporate strategy. How interlinked are these businesses? If one is axed, will that affect competitiveness in another? What are the inter-business synergies? Is Extramural the best parent for each (see Tool 18)?

They conclude that the educational tour business could fare better under a different parent and so should fetch a good sale price. Proceeds will be reinvested into school activity tours and day camps, between which there are tangible cross-selling and marketing synergies.

The owners have developed a robust corporate strategy for Extramural.

Creating value through mergers, acquisitions and alliances

These tools will help you:

- Appreciate that most mergers, acquisitions and alliances (M&A) destroy value
- Understand how synergies drive value creation in M&A
- Walk away from the wrong deal

About these tools

Eat or be eaten.

This old adage may have pejorative undertones, but it does serve as a reminder of the dangers of corporate underperformance.

Mergers, acquisitions and alliances have been with us since the dawn of capitalism. They form an important, if on occasion controversial, component of the Anglo-Saxon business model.

M&A are frequently deemed to be successful when the merged entity survives, yet all too often they have, in reality, failed, as defined in the only truly meaningful manner: the creation of incremental shareholder value.

At the very least, the shareholder value of AB should be greater that the stand-alone pre-merger value of A plus the stand-alone pre-merger value of B.

But studies are regularly carried out, since well before I started working on M&A activities in the mid-1980s, which show, again and again, that, **in the majority of cases**, shareholder value is destroyed by M&A, not enhanced.

The reason is simple: acquirers pay too much to gain control.

And the reasons behind that over-payment are also well known:

▪ Managers are often hell-bent on closing the deal – they have set their minds on it, for whatever reason, genuinely strategic or personal empire building (and pay packet boosting), and they are damned if they will permit prolonged negotiations and an ever-rising price tag to prevent them from so doing

▪ Managers do insufficient strategic analysis pre-deal along the lines set out in this tool

▪ Managers underestimate the difficulties of post-deal integration and the inevitable delay in achieving aspired merger benefits.

The theory behind M&A value creation is simple. We start with the premise that acquisition of company B by A will be of strategic benefit to A. Then:

▪ The acquisition will create synergies, i.e. benefits in cost saving or revenue enhancement that will be tapped by the joining forces of A and B

▪ The value of AB will exceed the stand-alone values of A and B by the value of the synergies

▪ Company A will be unable to buy B at its stand-alone value – shareholders of B will demand a premium to the pre-bid price to cede control

▪ The acquisition will be successful, as defined by creating, not destroying, value for the shareholders of A, if the synergy value is greater than the premium paid by A for B.

The challenge of this M&A tool, therefore, is to work out the synergy value.

How to use them

There are six tasks in the acquisition assessment process:

- Confirm strategic rationale
- Select the right target
- Assess the risks
- Value the stand-alone entities
- Value the net synergies
- Ensure added value.

More detail follows.

Confirm strategic rationale

Very often the acquisition of a business happens opportunistically, so the temptation is to move straight to due diligence.

The temptation should be resisted. Acquisition is a time-consuming and resource-hungry business. You can't be doing half a dozen at a time.

Take a step backwards and confirm the strategic rationale – and in the light of that rationale, assess whether this potential target really is the most promising candidate.

There are three steps in the task of confirming strategic rationale:

1 What are your strategic objectives?
2 Is acquisition the appropriate route?
3 What are your transferable strengths?

Taking one at a time. . .

1 What are your strategic objectives?

Reviews of the rationale for acquisitions are frequent and tend to point to these main objectives:

- Access new markets/products
- Acquire skills/technologies
- Achieve economies
- Spread risk
- Reduce competition.

Motivation for acquisition can be offensive, defensive (e.g. if your objective is to reduce competition) or a mix. What are yours?

2 Is acquisition the appropriate route?

There are four broad alternative routes to achieving your business objectives, with pros and cons for each – see Table 17.1. Is acquisition the best route for you?

Table 17.1 The strategic rationale for acquisition

Route	Pros		Cons	
Organic	Strategic clarity	Control	Investment	Time
Acquisition	Time	Control	Investment premium	Integration
Merger	Time	Little investment	Shared control	Integration/management
Alliance	Time	Little investment	Shared control	Integration/management

3 What are your transferable strengths?

Here you should identify your transferable strengths – and any constraining weaknesses. This should be a guide to identifying and assessing realisable synergies later on in the process.

Your transferable strengths may be in R&D, operational efficiency, marketing, distribution coverage, financial control. One classic example a good few years ago was in the application of Nestlé's marketing and distribution strengths to the quality product range of Rowntree – a rationale repeated, albeit more controversially, by Kraft in its acquisition of Cadbury in 2010.

Select the right target

The second task is to select the right target, for which there are four steps:

1 Set criteria for strategic fit

2 Prioritise the criteria

3 Screen the candidates rigorously

4 Rank the candidates.

Taking one at a time. . .

1 Set criteria for strategic fit

Criteria are best divided in two – hard and soft criteria – to ensure that the soft criteria get adequate attention.

Examples of hard criteria are size, product/market segments, technologies, competitive capabilities and financial standing.

The criteria need to reflect your objectives for the acquisition. If your main rationale is to acquire skills, for example, you will be looking for a target that is strong in those skills you want to acquire. To enhance your bargaining position, however, you probably will want a target that is weak in those skills where you are strong. If, on the other hand, your rationale is to achieve economies of scale, you will want to be sure that the target has a strong competitive position in key segments.

The soft criteria for strategic fit may be equally important. These may include orientation towards customers or employees. Or the firm's culture concerning innovation, or cost control.

Remember, the greater the difference in the 'cultural map' between the two organisations, the more difficult the post-transaction integration is likely to be. Ideally, you and your target will share a common business philosophy. If you don't, you may need to factor the differences into your later assessments on synergy benefits.

2 Prioritise the criteria

Now you need to set priorities. The essential criteria, the ones the target has to meet if there is to be any point in going ahead with the deal, will be your 'screening criteria'. Applying them to all potential targets will allow you to eliminate the non-starters quickly. The 'nice to have' criteria will help you rank the companies that pass through the initial screening in order of attractiveness.

This two-stage process is important if you are to end up with the right target. In a one-stage ranking process, there is a danger that you could end up with a target that scores high on all but one criterion, which would be a screening criterion in a two-stage process. It is better to have a two-stage process and find a target that ranks reasonably in the ranking criteria but passes through the screening.

Differing criteria may have differing weighting depending on the precise nature of the deal. In an outright acquisition, a common business philosophy can be helpful, but not necessarily essential. In an acquisition with an ongoing relationship component, i.e. a form of alliance, a common business philosophy may well be critical, hence a screening criterion.

3 Screen the candidates rigorously

The next step in finding the right target is to screen all the potential candidates. Be ruthless. If any candidate fails to meet every one of your screening criteria, drop it from your list. Those that pass through the screen move on to the ranking stage – see Figure 17.1.

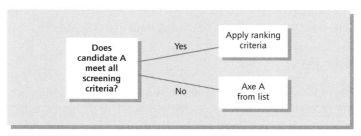

Figure 17.1 Screening acquisition candidates for fit

4 Rank the candidates

Suppose you have four candidates that have passed through the screening stage: A, B, C and D. Now you rank them – see Table 17.2.

Table 17.2 Ranking acquisition candidates for fit and availability

				Candidates		
Criteria for fit		Weight	A	B	C	D
Hard	Segment attractiveness	20	3	3	4	3
	Segment strategic fit	10	4	3	3	3
	Business strategic fit	30	3	3	2.5	4
Soft	Business cultural fit	40	3	4	2	3
Overall rating for fit (0–5)		100	3.1	3.4	2.6	3.3
Overall ranking for fit			3	1	4	2
Availability			X	Y	Y	YY

First you weight the ranking criteria in relative importance – in the example, cultural fit is given a high weighting.

Next you rank the candidates by each criterion, with B emerging as the best bet.

Then you compare the ranking with an assessment of availability: in the case above, it seems a toss-up between the preferred candidate B and the more available D. It's probably best to start talking to both.

The same process must be applied if you are approached by an interested potential target: be careful, it may be candidate C!

Assess the risks

There should be no substitute for the process of due diligence. Many acquisitions have succeeded without it, or without much of it, but that has been down to luck. They could have been disasters.

Without financial due diligence, the target's management accounts may be misleading. Without legal due diligence, don't be surprised if you receive a letter from a lawyer representing some aggrieved claimant soon after signing. Without environmental due diligence, how can you be sure of the target's compliance with regulation?

Above all, though you could argue I would say this, since I have specialised in the field since the mid-1980s, it is strategic due diligence that will give you the answers to the fundamental question: will this deal create or destroy shareholder value?

To be able to value the synergies, you need to know at what rate the market is growing, how competitive forces are impacting on pricing, how the target is positioned relative to competitors, how positioning is set to change – not least of which as a result of this merger, what will be the impact of recent and planned business initiatives by the target, and so forth. All this needs to be done for each major product/market segment (if the target is a business) or each business unit (if the target is a multi-business corporation).

The risks and opportunities identified by the due diligence need to be assessed by likelihood of occurrence and likely impact on value should they occur – see the Suns & Clouds Chart of Tool 25.

You then need to build key risks and opportunities into your cash-flow forecasts for the target. By attaching probabilities against each key risk or opportunity occurring, you can derive expected value cash-flow forecasts, hence the stand-alone value of the target.

Value the stand-alone entities

Discounted cash-flow (DCF) analysis is by far the best tool for valuation, but there are many pitfalls awaiting the novice user and you may prefer to use more rough-and-ready valuation techniques, such as these three:

■ Net asset value – but this is a book (historic), not market, valuation and typically understates value, often by some distance.

■ Comparable trading multiples – you can find relevant
multiples of publicly traded companies operating off the Web;
sales, EBITDA, EBIT or P/E multiples are used most frequently –
but they all suffer from the same shortcoming, in that they are
multiples of the trading performance of one company during
one period of time, which may or may not be indicative of
trend performance.

■ Comparable transaction multiples – you can search various
databases for sales or earnings multiples on deals completed
in the last few years, where the targets have operated in the
same or similar industry sectors, but again these multiples
will refer to specific time points in history, when both trading
performance and the appetite for acquiring stock in that
sector might differ from today.

My advice is to use all three techniques above to value a company
to around a certain range, hopefully not too broad and within +/–
15 per cent of the central point.

Then try DCF analysis on the company, forecasting revenues and
costs to get profits and fixed and working capital expenditure to
get cash flow, before discounting back to values of today. Tweak
assumptions within reason and try a range of (reasonable) discount rates before you reach a net present value (NPV) around
and about the central point derived from the three rough-and-
ready valuation techniques.

This will give you a set of cash flows with which you can do
some sensitivity testing in step 3 to derive synergy values. They
will be estimates, but should be usable – and very much better
than nothing.

Value the target on a stand-alone basis

Based on the target's financial information disclosed to you in
the confidential information memorandum, or in greater detail
in the online data room, draw up a base-case set of cash-flow forecasts for the target.

The forecasts should show revenues and direct (and preferably
variable overhead) costs for each major product/market segment.

Derive a central value for the target using the techniques outlined above.

Value your firm on a stand-alone basis

Do the same for your firm, or at least for those product/market segments, or business units, that will be inter-relating with the target following acquisition. Use the same discount rate as for the target.

Value the net synergies

First you need to identify the synergies to be gained from merging two companies, then you need to value them.

Identify the synergies

M&A synergies are best identified under three areas:

- Revenue enhancement synergies
- Operating cost savings
- Capital cost savings.

Revenue enhancement synergies typically come from these areas:

- The target selling your product (or service) to its customers
- You selling the target's product to your customers
- You and the target combining to sell new product to both sets of customers
- Your combined capabilities enabling you to sell more or different product to your customers or to reach new customers
- But don't forget the negative synergies – those customers, possibly shared, you may lose due to their shifting some or all purchases to a third supplier.

Operating cost savings are often the main rationale for acquisition. Savings can come from one or many of these areas:

- Lower cost of raw materials or components due to greater purchasing power
- Likewise of outsourced services, such as IT or payroll
- Economies of scale in production

- Economies of scope
- Rationalisation of overhead staff, whether in sales, marketing or administration
- Rationalisation of physical assets – buildings, land, factories, offices, plant, equipment.

Finally, capital cost savings can be realised often on acquisition. Instead of building an extension to your factory, acquisition of a competitor with spare capacity can provide you with the space and, hopefully, the right equipment to maintain growth. Likewise, capital cost savings can be in the field of IT, head office or the like.

Value the net synergies

You have a DCF model of the target. Now make specific assumptions on each of the revenue enhancement synergies identified above. By how much will sales of product X grow each year with promotion to the target's customers?

By how much has the target's NPV increased? That is the value of that particular synergy.

And how about product Y?

And what about selling the target's product Z to **your** customers? By how much has the NPV of your firm increased from the stand-alone valuation you did earlier?

Work out the value of each revenue enhancement synergy.

Then do the same for each cost-saving synergy.

Add them up and you have a number for total synergy value. But wait! There are two big caveats:

- Managers tend to overestimate the magnitude of synergies, often wildly so; it is in the nature of the M&A process – the thrill of the chase. Apply a 50 per cent probability factor to your revenue enhancement synergies (say, R), to give an expected value of 0.5R; likewise, apply an 80 per cent probability to all cost savings (C) – which are more in your control and ability to influence – to give an expected value of 0.8C.

▨ Don't forget the transaction costs pre-deal and the costs of integrating the two companies post-deal – not just in redundancies, but in such items as early lease termination.

You now have a base estimate of the value of the net synergies from this transaction.

Ensure added value

You now have three sets of data:

▨ A base estimate of the stand-alone value of the target

▨ A base estimate of the synergy value of the acquisition

▨ An assessment of risk and opportunity.

Acquisition premiums tend to be in the range 30–40 per cent. If that is what you are likely to have to pay and if your base estimate of the synergy value of the acquisition is less than 40 per cent of that of the stand-alone value of the target, you should walk away.

If synergy value is higher than that, you need to consider the risks and opportunities identified and assessed during due diligence. If any risks are sufficiently likely to make a big dent in either the stand-alone value of the target or in the synergies (or both), you may need to walk away.

Again, remember: more than half of all acquisitions destroy value. This is because the acquirer overpaid.

You don't want to be part of that statistic.

When to use them – or be wary

In a merger, acquisition or alliance, an approach such as this is essential.

Be wary of each such transaction. One last time: most fail!

Alliances have an even higher failure rate. An alliance, whether a simple marketing relationship or a full joint venture, is an inherently unstable vehicle. The partners need to work together in harmony for the good of the alliance, but sometimes to the detriment or neglect of the parent company's interests.

They require even more pre-deal strategic analysis than in an acquisition. The process is very similar (differences are in bold):

- Confirm strategic rationale
- Select the right **partner**
- Assess the risks
- Value **each partner's contribution**
- Value the net synergies
- Ensure added value.

Unlike in an acquisition, **both parties** need to emerge from the pre-deal process believing they have secured a reasonable deal. Otherwise the alliance will be off to a lopsided start and its prospects for longevity will be minimal.

But they can work to add shareholder value and they can be long-lasting. The alliances that are Unilever and Royal Dutch Shell are their embodiment, but a clear example of a successful, more recent joint venture is Cereal Partners Worldwide (CPW). From its formation in 1990, as a full frontal assault on the pre-eminence of Kellogg's in Europe, it looked like a winning, almost obvious strategy – the realisation perhaps of Kellogg's' worst nightmare. The combination of General Mills, the other cereal giant in the USA, with the marketing clout of Nestlé and, two decades on, CPW has become, all but inevitably, a formidable player in the European cereal market.

---

case study

Using it: Lloyds Banking Group

I have banked with Lloyds all my life. I remember with fondness the days when the local bank manager would send round a member of

▶

➤ his staff to help my father with counting the takings on the first day of a sale at his ladies fashion store in West Wales. Even in later, less personal years, it always seemed a reasonable bank, unspectacular, but steady.

I was also, foolishly, in retrospect, a long-term shareholder.

On 15 September 2008, one of the world's largest investment banks, Lehman Brothers, filed for Chapter 11 bankruptcy protection. The impact on global financial markets was devastating. Bank share prices tumbled, dragging non-financial shares down in their wake, depositors queued in the streets to pull out their funds, and governments piled in with loans and equity to shore up bank balance sheets.

One bank, HBOS, experienced exceptional turbulence in its share price in the aftermath of the Lehman bombshell. Yet, within days, amidst financial turmoil unprecedented since the 1930s, Lloyds Bank announced that it had reached agreement to acquire HBOS.

True, Lloyds had been eyeing this target for a couple of years, so presumably had run the slide rule over the target a few times beforehand.

But the financial world was in chaos – less so, perhaps, for Halifax, the former building society, than for Bank of Scotland, the other half of HBOS and renowned over the previous decade as one of the most adventurous banks in leveraged financial transactions.

If ever there were a time for cool heads and considered due diligence, it was then. Above all else, HBOS's loan book needed the most forensic investigation. As revealed by the Parliamentary Commission on Banking Standards of March 2013, HBOS's provision for bad loans was £370 million at the time of acquisition.

The final tab for bad loans, picked up by Lloyds' shareholders, over and above their £12 billion cost of acquisition, was £25 billion.

If you had £1,000 invested in Lloyds in early 2007, that would have contracted during the subsequent credit crunch and Lehman's collapse to around £500 by mid-September 2008 – which was fair enough, since that was happening to all banks. The news of the HBOS acquisition was greeted, however, with such concern that the Lloyds ➤

share price carried on tumbling. Six months post-acquisition, your investment would have been worth £70.

Even then the horror show wasn't over. Your investment would have reached a nadir of £40 around November 2011, before finally embarking on an upward trend to around £140 at the time of writing in March 2014.

If, instead, you had invested £1,000 in Barclays in early 2007, you would have received regular dividends and your investment would still be worth £320. If you had invested in HSBC, it would still be worth £650.

And it is not just investors who lost out from the ill-advised acquisition, but customers, too. The EU was unhappy with how the Gordon Brown government flagrantly flouted anti-trust laws during the takeover and forced Lloyds Banking Group to shed some of its branches, so Lloyds resuscitated its TSB brand.

This was a huge inconvenience to some customers, almost a farce. My personal accounts were moved to another branch of Lloyds and my business accounts, along with my wife's personal accounts, transferred to TSB. All without our consent. It took months of inconvenience and aggravation to unravel and return to the former situation.

In the press release issued to the Stock Exchange on 18 September 2008, Lloyds Bank stated: 'The acquisition is a compelling combination which offers substantial benefits for shareholders and customers.' Ha, ha.

If you are a non-executive director on the board of a company proposing an acquisition, may I suggest you start off with a 'Margaret Thatcher', namely 'No, no, no!' Only then let yourself be persuaded – gradually, painstakingly, after thorough, detailed, unhurried, coherent, credible, convincing, commercial and financial analysis – to sign off on the deal.

18

Creating parent value (Goold, Campbell and Alexander)

This tool will help you:

- Assess whether the businesses in your multi-business company are in the right home – or might be better off with another parent

- Judge whether a business belonging to a competitor might be better off with you as a parent

- Learn how your corporate HQ can become a better parent

About this tool

'To lose one parent may be regarded as a misfortune; to lose both looks like carelessness.'

The success of management buy-outs since the mid-1980s suggests that the converse to Oscar Wilde's quip can apply in the world of business. Losing a parent often has been far from unfortunate – it can liberate the offspring and spur them to thrive.

The Ashridge Strategic Management Centre has led the field in researching the management of multi-business companies. The 1994 book, *Corporate-Level Strategy: Creating Value in the Multi-Business Company*, written by three of their academics, Michael Goold, Andrew Campbell and Marcus Alexander, found that head office, or the corporate centre, more often than not failed to create value in a multi-business company. It destroyed value.

Goold et al. encourage the strategist to think of the centre as the intermediary between the investor and the business unit. The centre can add value to the business unit if there are net synergies between them, offsetting dissynergies such as:

- Wrong decision making by the centre due to distance from the front line and often unfamiliarity with the business unit's market environment and key success factors
- The demotivating aspect of distancing front-line managers from their investors
- The overhead expense of HQ, often high
- The acquisition premium, where the business was bought rather than organically built, and which is frequently way too high (see Tool 17).

They believe that multi-business companies can create synergistic value by developing the right 'parenting skills', exploiting the right 'parenting opportunities' and establishing a 'parenting advantage' by owning the business.

In essence, the centre, or 'parent', should view its business units using the same lens as the acquirer of Tool 17 – to create value, there should be synergies not just between businesses but between centre and business unit. That will create a parenting advantage.

They go further. If a parent's ownership of a business creates an advantage but a competing parent would create a bigger advantage, the parent should consider selling the business at a healthy sale premium and invest the proceeds in a business where the parenting advantage is maximised.

Successful parents have three key parenting characteristics:

- **Value-creation insights** – they have identified a mechanism for creating value common to many of their businesses – thus the identification of a common technology base by leading electronics manufacturers or the sprinkling of Virgin's stardust brand.

▨ **Distinctive parenting capabilities** – they are leaders in specific capabilities that are helping to deliver the value-creation insights and are transferable from parent to business – thus, the corporate R&D functions of many pharmaceutical groups or Virgin's centre leveraging brand promotion across all its businesses, by, for example, sponsoring a big city marathon.

▨ **Presence of 'heartland' businesses** – ownership of those businesses that are best placed to exploit the parent's value-creation insights and its distinctive parenting capabilities – thus the presence in Virgin Group of a mobile phone or banking business rather than a business-to-business engineering business.

How to use it

Ask these questions of the businesses in your firm's portfolio:

▨ Do the parenting opportunities in a business fit with the firm's value-creating insights and distinctive parenting capabilities?

▨ Do the key success factors (KSFs) in the business have any clear misfit with the firm's parenting characteristics?

See where each of your businesses sits on the Goold et al. parenting-fit matrix (Figure 18.1). They suggest five categories:

▨ **Heartland business** – where there is a strong fit between parenting characteristics and opportunities and also with the KSFs in the business

▨ **Edge-of-heartland business** – partial fit between parenting characteristics and opportunities and also KSFs: some fit, some don't; net value creation is marginal and you should consider how you could better boost performance against KSFs

▨ **Ballast business** – little fit between parenting characteristics and opportunities but no serious misfit with KSFs, a typical portfolio business that may well do better under a more synergistic parent; too many ballasts in your firm and you'll be a takeover target

▓ **Alien territory business** – a total misfit, from every perspective, your firm is destroying value there, exit fast

▓ **Value trap business** – a red flag business, where there is strong fit between parenting characteristics and opportunities, but a misfit with the KSFs of that business; the danger here is in you mistaking this business for an edge-of-heartland business – it is not, because your firm is not best placed to exploit the KSFs in this business.

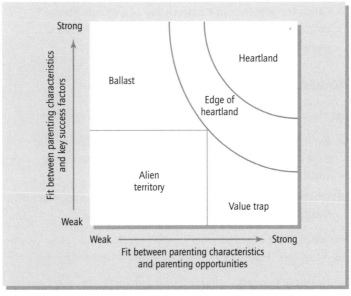

Figure 18.1 The parenting-fit matrix

Source: Adapted from Michael Goold, Andrew Campbell and Marcus Alexander, *Corporate-Level Strategy: Creating Value in the Multi-Business Company*, Wiley, 1994

Your portfolio ideally should consist of heartland businesses, or those on the edge, poised to be nudged into the heartland.

When to use it – or be wary

This tool forces you to think through the strategic rationale of why your firm's portfolio of businesses is as it is, how you add value to each business as a parent, building on your core competences (Tool 19), and how you can deploy these parental resources or capabilities to better create value in the future.

Don't fall into the trap of redefining your parent characteristics to justify a parenting opportunity – or even of asserting that you plan to strengthen the former to justify the latter. Parenting characteristics are harder to build than opportunities. It may be wiser to let the opportunity pass, or divest a business, than attempt to build a characteristic. It is easier to change the portfolio to fit the characteristic than vice versa.

---

case study

Using it: Energy companies and their mineral subsidiaries

A classic, well-researched example of parental value destruction was highlighted by Goold, Campbell and Alexander in their 1994 work.

Flush with cash following the oil crisis of the early 1970s, many of the oil majors ventured into the minerals market, typically through acquisition. They figured that the exploration and extraction of mineral resources would draw on the same set of skills needed in the oil business.

While this may have been true to a certain extent, the oil majors proved, in the main, to be poor parents. There were subtle differences in the businesses and the oil executives seemed unable to pick up on the nuances.

The impact on performance was extraordinary. In the mid-1980s, the mineral divisions of the oil majors Atlantic Richfield, BP, Shell, Exxon and Standard Oil achieved an average return on sales of –17 per cent.

In the same period, the average return on sales of the independent mineral companies was a positive 10 per cent.

The oil majors' mineral businesses would have fared better under different ownership. To return to Oscar Wilde: to lose a parent may be regarded as a misfortune, to gain a wrong 'un looks like carelessness.

Core competences
(Hamel and Prahalad)

This tool will help you:

- Recognise that corporate HQ has a role to play in nurturing the core competences needed for success across each business unit
- Reshape those core competences to forge new businesses
- Convey strategic intent throughout your organisation

About this tool

What are your firm's core competences?

If strategic thought was dominated in the 1970s by BCG's experience curve (Tool 14) and growth/share matrix (Tool 12) and in the 1980s by Michael Porter's Five Forces (Tool 6), the 1990s can be viewed in retrospect as the time of the resource-based school of corporate strategy.

Chief trumpeters of this school were Gary Hamel and C.K. Prahalad, culminating in their pioneering and influential book,

Competing for the Future, in 1994, but other business academics made arguably as important contributions. One, encountered already in Tool 8, was Grant's resources and capabilities strengths/importance matrix.

Hamel and Prahalad believed fervently that there was more to corporate strategy than just portfolio planning. Corporate HQ had a major role to play in areas such as developing strengths in key operational processes (termed 'core competences') and conveying a sense of vision throughout the firm (termed 'strategic intent').

Instead of the downsizing or re-engineering prevalent at the time, companies should be 'reinventing their industry' or 'regenerating their strategy'. They proposed a new, radically more ambitious, strategy paradigm.

Table 19.1 shows just 6 of the 13 strategic challenges they set out, 6 that arguably have had much impact on subsequent strategic thinking. Of these, competing for leadership in core competences (or 'competencies' in their language) has been the most influential.

Table 19.1 Getting to the future first

Not only	But also
Competing for market share	Competing for opportunity share
Strategy as positioning	Strategy as foresight
Strategy as fit	Strategy as stretch: intent
Strategy as resource allocation	Strategy as resource leverage
Competing within an industry	Competing to reshape industry
Competing in products	Competing in core competences

Source: Adapted from Gary Hamel and C.K. Prahalad, *Competing for the Future,* Harvard Business School Press, 1994

The authors define a core competence as an 'integrated bundle of skills and technologies'. It represents the 'sum of learning across individual skill sets and individual organizational units'. It is unlikely to reside in a single individual or small team, and may not reside in a single business unit.

Core competences in financial services, for example, are quoted as relationship management, transaction processing, risk management, foreign exchange, financial engineering, trading skills, investment management, tele-service and customer information capture.

How to use it

Hamel and Prahalad see the key to competing for the future as the building, deploying, protecting and defending of your core competences.

They suggest you should draw up a chart of the core competences needed to compete in the market, distinguishing between those of today and of tomorrow – see Figure 19.1.

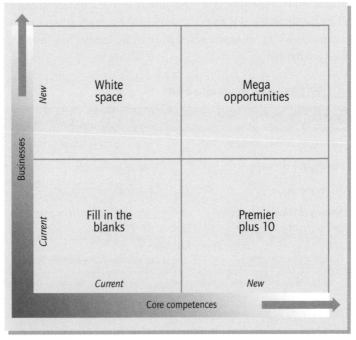

Figure 19.1   **Acquiring core competences**

Source: Adapted from Gary Hamel and C.K. Prahalad, *Competing for the Future*, Harvard Business School Press, 1994, 'Establishing the Core Competence Acquisition Agenda'

These are the key questions that emerge from the chart:

- In the lower-left quadrant, 'Fill in the blanks': representing your current portfolio of competences for your current businesses (or product/market segments – this tool can be used for business strategy, too), what is the opportunity to improve your position by better leveraging your current core competences?

- In the lower-right quadrant, 'Premier plus 10': to become the premier provider in 5 to 10 years' time, what new competences will you need to build, protect and defend your franchise in current markets?

- In the upper-left quadrant, 'White space': what new businesses (or segments) could you create by redeploying or recombining your existing core competences?

- In the upper-right quadrant, 'Mega opportunities': what new core competences would you need to build to participate in the most exciting businesses (segments) of the future?

The more distinctive, the more unique, the more defensible is your core competence, the more value it has.

How can you strengthen your core competences and thereby build value?

When to use it – or be wary

Use this tool in corporate strategy, when thinking what the corporate centre can do to add value to the business units. How can the centre help in building a core competence and ensuring its widespread application across all business units?

Michael Porter is one of many who believe that a firm's value resides at business level ('corporations don't compete, business units do') and the role of corporate should be no more than resource allocator. Hamel and Prahalad might respond by saying that successful companies leverage their core competences across all business units and, anyway, their model works just as well at the business unit level.

Other critiques of the core competence model focus on the difficulty of deciding on what is or is not a core competence. Unlike a tangible asset, it is difficult to measure and managers may overinflate the firm's worthiness for their own agenda. This is a criticism applied likewise to the attractiveness/advantage matrix (Tool 11) and suggests that a degree of objective oversight, along with a rigorous customer survey and benchmarking exercise, might be beneficial in the application of the model. It does not invalidate it.

---

case study

Using it: Red Bull

There is, in Southeast Asia, a massive, black, bison-type creature with a prominent curved ridge on its back, drooped shoulders and ferocious curved horns. This endangered bovine is a gaur and it proved an inspirational name for the energy drink created by Chaleo Yoovidhya, a Thai pharmaceutical businessman.

His concoction was a stimulating concentration of ingredients, such as sugar, caffeine, taurine and vitamins, and soon developed a reputation for keeping the body alert and awake, becoming particularly popular with Thai truck drivers. *Krating Daeng* (red gaur) was pitched squarely at the common man and launch promotion included sponsorship of Muay Thai, the hugely popular Thai boxing, which combines assault with feet and elbows, as well as fists.

An Austrian marketer, Dietrich Mateschitz, came across the drink on a business trip to Thailand, spotted the promise and linked up with Chaleo to take the brand international. He launched Red Bull in his home country on 1 April 1987 with the rather cumbersome tag line 'Red Bull: so awesome that the polka dots will literally fly off your tie'!

But, within a year, Red Bull had found its marketing sweet spot, sponsoring the Dolomitenmann (man of the Dolomites, a mountain range in northeastern Italy) – a marathon endurance event combining mountain running, paragliding, kayaking and mountain biking. Soon Red Bull was to sponsor Flugtag (fly day) in Vienna, a whacky event where teams competed to launch home-made, human-powered, creative and/ or flashy flying machines – later to be rolled out in over 40 countries. The die was cast, as was the tagline: 'Red Bull gives you wings'.

▶ Red Bull's market positioning has been ruthlessly consistent. If an extreme or endurance sport exists, especially if it relates to flight, or at least speed, it will sponsor either the event or a team (or an individual). Thus it started its own Formula 1 team in 2005 and was rewarded with three successive victories for both driver Sebastian Vettel and constructors in 2010–12 (although its venture into NASCAR racing proved less successful, resulting in team withdrawal in 2011).

If an extreme sport didn't exist, Red Bull invented it. Thus the Red Bull Crashed Ice in Stockholm (racing on hockey skates down an ice track with obstacles and jumps), the Red Bull X-Fighters in Valencia (motocross-cum-bullfighting!) or the Red Bull X-Alps, where masochistic athletes hike and/or paraglide over an extraordinary 1,200-mile journey from Austria to Monaco!

Or they moved from old to new. In 1999, Red Bull sponsored the B.A.S.E. jumper Felix Baumgartner to leap off the world's then tallest building, Petronas Towers in Kuala Lumpur, where he broke the then record for longest free fall (eight seconds) and fastest speed achieved (105 mph). Thirteen years later, Red Bull sponsored the same daredevil to leap from the edge of space, 128,000 feet above ground, and 8 million people watched live on YouTube, and 30 million later, as Baumgartner became to the first individual to travel at supersonic speed, namely 833.9 mph!

As an example of sustained market positioning, the persistent reinforcement of the message 'Red Bull gives you wings', backed up by targeted sponsorship of events that purport to do just that, Red Bull is hard to beat. It is Red Bull's core competence. The message has powered sales reaching 5.5 billion cans in 2013.

What next for the company – a red gaur jumping over the moon, while the dish runs away with the spoon?

20

Deliberate and emergent strategy (Mintzberg)

This tool will help you:

- To not be enslaved to strategic planning
- Realise that sometimes, and in some sectors, things move too fast
- Listen to your line managers, carry out pilot projects, tease the market

About this tool

'And now for something completely different,' Monty Python might say here. Having set out, in the last few tools, the main proponents of the market-based and resource-based schools of strategy, we turn to an iconoclast – Henry Mintzberg of McGill University.

Is all this strategising a waste of time? Worse, could it steer a company in the wrong direction, lead to wrong decisions, wrong actions?

Is strategic planning too restrictive, too structured, too analytical, too centralised, done by too many people, clever, yes, but unbloodied, unexposed to the front line?

Would strategy not be better conducted by line managers, responding to events as they unfold, as they see them, taking risks, testing the market, probing for opportunities?

Strategy should be as much emergent as deliberate, says Mintzberg (see Figure 20.1). Strategic planning remains useful, but it needs to be:

▪ More decentralised

▪ More intuitive.

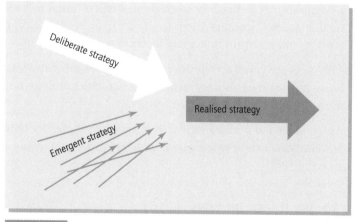

Figure 20.1 **Deliberate and emergent strategies**

Source: Adapted from *The Rise and Fall of Strategic Planning* by Mintzberg, H. Pearson Education Limited © 2000 Pearson Education Limited.

It is better done by managers than strategists. Five-year plans can be out of date inside a couple of years in mature industries or before the ink has dried in technology industries.

Industry boundaries have become more fluid. The value chain is more dispersed and more shared. Unusual events, foreseeable only in retrospect, throw plans off course more frequently. Industry analysis can be redundant, even misleading.

Firms need to be fleet of foot, strategically flexible. Organisations need to be structured as an 'adhocracy', the diametric opposite of a bureaucracy, with flat lines of responsibility, decentralised decision making and small-team project work, with appropriate liaison mechanisms.

Strategy should emerge over time as intentions collide with and respond to a changing reality.

This is emergent strategy. It is what works in practice.

How to use it

Be cognisant of the need for strategic flexibility. Listen to your line managers. Encourage them to think about how unfolding events are impacting on strategy. Be aware of emergent strategy.

Don't necessarily wait for the next planning process to grind into gear, especially in technology sectors. Carry out pilot projects, test for markets here and there. Suck it and see.

Adapt and amend strategy, as required, as you go along, but only if a sound case can be made – perhaps in retrospect, following a successful pilot.

When to use it – or be wary

The more change you witness in your market, the more strategy should evolve. But whether that should result in a succession of deliberate strategies or a shift towards emergent strategy is your call for your organisational culture.

Emergent strategy is no substitute for deliberate strategy. Taken to its extreme, emergent strategy equals no strategy, just flying by the seat of the pants.

Yes, industry boundaries can become fluid, yes, value chains are less rigid. But this is not new and these changes mostly take time. The future market environment can be envisioned. Your strategy can be deliberate.

Yes, there are what Nassim Nicholas Taleb terms 'black swan' events – in recent years we have had EU sovereign debt, the banking collapse, Fukushima, Deepwater Horizon, Katrina, 9/11 – and these have, indeed, blown the strategic plans of many companies.

But this has ever been the case. For the sovereign debt crisis, read the Latin American debt crisis, the shipping debt crisis, the LBO debt crisis, the dot-com bust of earlier years. Or go back further to the South Sea Bubble.

Strategy is not set in stone. It responds and evolves.

Read Mintzberg; he is a breath of fresh air. Here is his spiel on the back cover of *Strategy Bites Back*: 'OK, strategy is crucial. We all know that. But why must it be so deadly serious? So plodding, uncreative, **boring**? Dull strategy books create dull strategists that produce dull strategies that fail. Now here's an antidote.'

If so inspired, let your strategy be emergent!

P.S. Mark Maletz and Nitin Nohria followed similar lines to Mintzberg in their research on 'white space', the 'large but mostly unoccupied territory in every company where rules are vague, authority is fuzzy, budgets are non-existent, and strategy is unclear – and where entrepreneurial activity that helps reinvent and renew an organisation most often takes place'. They describe how senior executives nurture white-space projects by putting aside the traditional planning, organising and controlling techniques deployed in the 'black space'. In effect, they let the strategy emerge.

---

case study

Using it: Facebook

It is said in the electronic world that 'the early bird gets the worm, but the second mouse gets the cheese'. There were plenty of cheesy smiles on the faces of Facebook staff on IPO day, May 2012.

In all the hype, and a valuation in excess of $100 billion, one existential question seemed to have been sidelined: will someone do to Facebook what Facebook did to MySpace?

Facebook took out MySpace because, to mix metaphors, it invented a better mousetrap. It rapidly became an online social networking site that was multi-generational, multi-purpose, multi-functional and multi-corporate.

Some claim that this success was due to the pursuit of an unadulterated Mintzberg-cum-white-space philosophy, with little strategising and, instead, ceaseless piloting of new ideas. Perhaps, but the extent to which systems developed where new ideas were quickly tested and summarily planned pre-pilot is difficult to deconstruct in such a fast-growing environment.

The example of Facebook suggests that the faster-moving the environment the more progress a firm will make if it has a flat, entrepreneurial, relatively unplanned and rule-free, innovative, Mintzbergian environment. But that's assuming they make the right calls...

And what of the future? Could someone new come in with something slightly different, something fresher? Something cooler?

Could China's WeChat or Japan's Line, both instant-messaging/ photo-sharing apps combined with social networking, cross borders? Already Line is dominating the market in Thailand, posing a threat to Facebook and Twitter. It is now taking on WhatsApp in the test battleground of Spain.

Should a usurper arrive, the tipping point could be sudden and catastrophic. The barriers to switching are minimal. The risks are high. To many, the IPO valuation of Facebook defied economic logic.

Profit from the core (Zook)

This tool will help you:

- Encourage your firm to stay focused and pursue growth opportunities within your core business...

- ...or in adjacent businesses where your strengths are transferable...

- ...or in pre-emptively redefining your core business

About this tool

Has your firm, like an overly curious cat, strayed too far from home?

Most growth strategies fail to deliver value because they venture too far, concluded Chris Zook, a partner at Bain & Company. The timeless strategic precept, that of building power in a well-defined core, remains the key source of competitive advantage and the most viable platform for successful expansion.

Successful companies operate in an F-E-R cycle:

- **F**ocus on, understand and reach full potential in the core business
- **E**xpand into logical adjacent businesses surrounding that core
- **R**edefine pre-emptively the core business in response to market turbulence.

These were the findings of a study of over 2,000 companies and interviews with over 100 CEOs by Bain & Company and summarised in Zook's 2001 book, *Profit from the Core*.

In other words, as advised by Tom Peters and Robert Waterman in their best-selling book of 1982, *In Search of Excellence*, stick to the knitting.

How to use it

First you need to identify your core. Consider the key assets in your firm – your most potentially profitable customers, your most strategic capabilities, your most critical product offerings, your most important channels and any other critical strategic assets such as patents or brand name.

Now consider these three strategic growth alternatives (see Figure 21.1):

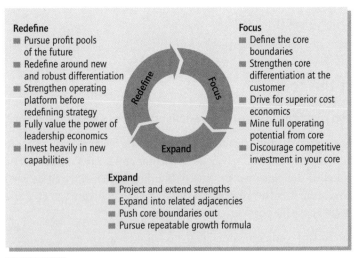

Redefine
- Pursue profit pools of the future
- Redefine around new and robust differentiation
- Strengthen operating platform before redefining strategy
- Fully value the power of leadership economics
- Invest heavily in new capabilities

Focus
- Define the core boundaries
- Strengthen core differentiation at the customer
- Drive for superior cost economics
- Mine full operating potential from core
- Discourage competitive investment in your core

Expand
- Project and extend strengths
- Expand into related adjacencies
- Push core boundaries out
- Pursue repeatable growth formula

Figure 21.1 **Profit from the core: the F-E-R cycle**

Source: Reprinted with permission from Chris Zook, *Unstoppable: finding hidden assets to renew the core and fuel profitable growth*, Harvard Business School Publishing, 2007

1 **Strengthen and defend the core.** Define business boundaries, confirm sources of differentiation and assess whether the core is functioning at or near full potential.

2　**Grow through adjacencies.** Consider expansion into adjacent markets that utilise and preferably reinforce your strengths in the profitable core.

3　**Redefine your core business.** Consider whether you need to redefine your core business – is this the right time, what methods work best, what lessons can be learnt from past successes or failures?

Be careful in defining adjacencies. Zook stresses that adjacency expansion differs from other growth strategies in its use of existing customer relationships, technologies or core business skills to build competitive advantage in a new area.

Map out your growth opportunities. Here is one process example in mapping adjacencies:

■ Rank your cores from strongest to weakest based on economics and relative competitive strength, as well as richness of adjacent growth opportunity

■ Develop the adjacencies in greater detail, considering new products, new markets, new businesses, new capabilities or vertical integration – see Figure 21.2

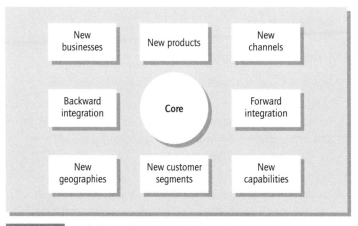

Figure 21.2　**Profit from the core: exploring adjacencies**

Source: Reprinted with permission from Chris Zook, *Profit from the Core*, Harvard Business Press, 2001

- Rank adjacency opportunities by size, strength of transferable advantage, competition, importance to core (offensive or defensive), coherence with long-term strategy and ability to implement
- Develop a cluster of moves or develop scenarios
- Draw up implementation plans.

When to use it – or be wary

Any time you find your strategy veering too far from your core business, think on Zook's F-E-R cycle and consider whether you would be better off in the Focus or Redefine stage or, if the Expand stage is where you are at, whether more adjacent opportunities can be exploited.

This is research-based, definitive affirmation of the dangers of woolly-thinking diversification and straying from your core business or core capabilities.

Arguably, there is little new here. The risks inherent in diversification were pointed out by Igor Ansoff decades earlier (Tool 10). But, as they say, it is not what one says but how and when one says it...

case study

Using it: Marvel Entertainment

Zook uses Marvel as a classic illustration of his 'profit from the core'.

In the mid-1990s, Marvel Entertainment looked down and out, filing for Chapter 11 bankruptcy protection. Comic books were a thing of the past – often sold in niche, whacky stores to aficionados as likely to be nostalgic baby boomers as today's teenagers.

But the company's core asset lay less in an outdated medium than in its content – the 5,000 characters themselves and their market-tested, customer-proven stories. A new CEO led the thrust into diversifying the medium, through movies, reinforced by merchandising and video games.

The movie *X-Men* launched with fanfare in 2000, followed by the even higher grossing *Spider-Man* in 2002. The bandwagon kept on rolling, the formula repeated through sequels and new character introductions such as *Wolverine* and the *Incredible Hulk*, and Marvel was sold to Disney in 2009 for $4 billion.

The company had profited from the core. Its transformation was a marvel.

Disruptive technologies (Christensen)

This tool will help you:

- Be wary of the inferior offering of a new competitor, which may have a single, attractive attribute sufficient to gain a beachhead

- Understand that, as the competitor improves performance and reduces cost, your market could be usurped

- Acknowledge the dilemma and invest in the lesser, disruptive technology, thereby cannibalising your existing, superior technology

About this tool

Great firms can fail by doing everything right.

All is going fine, then along comes a new technology, usually of inferior, seemingly retrogressive quality and hence resisted, even disparaged, by the firm and by its customers, and all is disrupted – says Clayton Christensen.

Christensen's 1997 book, *The Innovator's Dilemma: When New Technologies Cause Great Firms to Fail*, exploded onto the business world. Everyone knew of large firms being felled by new technologies, but this was research that showed that many of them had done nothing wrong to merit such a fall, strategically or managerially. They were doing what they should have done, not realising that their very successes and capabilities were obstacles to changing markets and technologies.

He sets out two types of technology: sustaining and disruptive. Established companies are adept at keeping abreast of the former, less so the latter. A sustaining technology is one that enhances an existing product, typically improving its performance and benefits to the customer. Successful established companies have processes that enable them to stay on top of these technologies, resulting in continuous product improvement and sustained customer satisfaction.

A disruptive technology is one that radically alters the benefit/price algorithm. Typically it produces a product of distinctly inferior quality or performance (though often smaller, simpler and/or more convenient), at least in the short term, but at such a lower price point that customers either rethink their rationale for purchasing the product or new customers are attracted into the market.

Examples abound – rail carriage producers lost out to saloon car manufacturers, Facit and Xerox to Canon, Olivetti to Amstrad, Concorde to Learjet, mainframe producers to mini-computers to personal computers to laptops to tablets/smart phone producers, offset to digital printers, Lucent to Cisco, Encyclopaedia Britannica to Wikipedia, music companies and CD producers to Apple's iTunes.

Christensen studied the hard disc industry in depth and found that established companies tended to lag two years or so behind newcomers coming in with a new, typically smaller, product generation. Seagate, leaders in the 5.25" disc, invented the 3.5" disc, but found little interest from their customers, who were happy with the status quo. Some Seagate employees left to form their own start-ups, producing the smaller disc, while Seagate continued to invest heavily in the larger disc, improving performance and sales. Over time the performance of the new smaller discs improved and started to displace the larger discs in the laptop and PC markets. Seagate belatedly fought back, but never reached the market share it had enjoyed in the larger disc market.

Two things from this research proved illuminating and not confined to hard discs:

- Barriers to technological change come as much from major customers as from within the major producers themselves – often what the customer says is what the producer wants to hear, so they can carry on with what they are doing
- Disruptive technologies are very often promoted by new players to the market, not constrained by old technologies, old processes, old positioning, old sales pitches and, importantly, as above, the old thinking of old customers.

Disruptive technologies succeed because they sneak in surreptitiously. They do not appeal to the top end of the market at first, due to their inferior product performance. Other attributes, such as size, simplicity or convenience, enable them to gain a beachhead in the market, from where they start to gain share either by improving performance or by driving cost down through the experience curve (Tool 14). Soon enough they dominate the market – see Figure 22.1.

This is what Christensen calls the 'innovator's dilemma'. At what stage does the innovator have to overcome cultural bias against the inferior product, both within and outside the firm, especially with customers, and embark on an investment programme with guaranteed cannibalisation of the firm's existing sales to protect against the possibility of an upstart doing the same thing?

A ubiquitous example of the innovator's dilemma is the world of e-commerce. Despite the huge advantages enjoyed by incumbent retailers, throughout the value chain, it is the upstarts who have dominated the market – the likes of Amazon, Gocompare, Trainline. It is only in food retailing (inevitably, due to the vastly different distribution challenges of the fresh, chilled and frozen food supply chain), banking (with its stability –formerly! – and

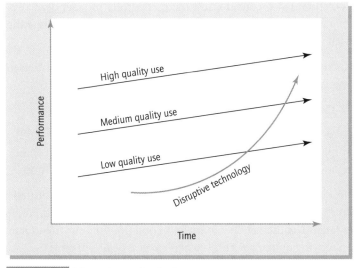

Figure 22.1 Disruptive technologies

Source: Adapted from Clayton M. Christensen, *The Innovator's Dilemma: When New Technologies Cause Great Firms to Fail*, Harvard Business School Press, 1997

security issues) and information (for example the BBC), where the 'bricks and clicks' model has worked.

How to use it

Solving the innovator's dilemma is easier said than done. Your challenge is to identify those emerging technologies that could threaten to steal share from or even supersede your current, sustaining technologies.

The trouble is, according to Christensen, that 'markets that don't exist can't be analysed'. Yes, to an extent, but that applies to any new venture – and one answer is to conduct pilot test marketing. Christensen suggests an alternative, discovery-driven planning, where you learn by doing and making real-time adjustments in strategy and planning. You should establish small, creative teams, bold and unafraid of failure, prepared to engage with freer-thinking customers on a range of what-if scenarios.

You should also consider setting up a wholly independent firm charged with exploiting the new technology, in effect competing with your sustained technologies.

If, on the other hand, you are the potential disruptor, Christensen says you should:

■ focus on core competences

■ consider what you need to excel at tomorrow to be successful

■ plan for the long term – and don't let short-term return on net assets (RONA) considerations drive key investment decisions.

'To make something simple and affordable is very complicated', says Christensen. 'When you make it affordable and simple, it enlarges the market. Try to make a good product but then focus on moving upmarket. This is where success begins or ends.'

When to use it – or be wary

Use this tool when you suspect new technologies may prove disruptive.

But stay within the bounds of probability – otherwise you will fritter away resources pursuing alternative technologies with minimal probability of them ever becoming disruptive.

---

case study

Using it: Toyota Motor Corporation

General Motors (GM) didn't pay too much heed to Toyota in the early days. The latter competed in the highly competitive, less profitable, smaller ('sub-compact') end of the market. Why bother to defend the least attractive, least profitable part of GM's business?

GM's resources were deployed more towards the larger, more upmarket, higher-margin segments of sedans, pickup trucks and sports utility vehicles.

By the time that GM realised the threat, consumers already had turned to the cheap, comfortable, reliable, Toyota sub-compacts in their droves, impacting adversely on sales at the lower end of the Chevrolet range.

By 2009 Toyota had peaked with a 17 per cent share of the US market, but a series of production problems and model recalls, including the marketer's nightmare of sticky gas pedals (an extraordinary turn of events for a company that hitherto had prided itself on uncompromising design and production excellence), saw them slip back to 14 per cent.

There were inroads, too, at the bottom end of the market from the Korean producers, Hyundai and Kia. Toyota's strategy now is to focus more on quality than share.

Disruptive technologies are not static – they evolve and repeat. Industry pundits foresee the day when Chinese sub-compacts will enter the USA and edge out the Koreans.

'Disruption keeps happening over and over again,' says Christensen. 'We have to have the ability to start new companies up. The only way for the leader who is being disrupted to catch the disruption is to create a completely different business unit and give it an unfettered charter to kill the parent.'

P.S. While writing this book, I happened across an article by Christine Lamb in *The Sunday Times* about a woman in a village in Afghanistan who had started working from home using a decrepit old sewing machine to make wedding and other dresses for special occasions. Nothing remarkable there, one might think, other than the fact that, under the former Taliban regime, women were not permitted to be engaged in the workforce in any way – certainly not in a workplace, not even from home. Their daughters were not even permitted to go to school. This woman has since acquired a bunch of other ancient sewing machines and now runs a business employing 16 seamstresses. It is a fabulous, heart-warming story, one of few to emerge from a country blighted by three decades of violence, but it did occur to me that it might not be such good news to the country's garment firms. A potentially disruptive technology?

Good strategy, bad strategy (Rumelt)

This tool will help you:

- Understand that bad strategy proliferates – it is all around us

- Realise that good strategy is rooted in three fundamentals – analytical diagnosis, a guiding policy on sustainable competitive advantage and its translation into action

- Implement good strategy through 'harnessing power'. . .

About this tool

'For many people in business, education and government the word "strategy" has become a verbal tic. A word that can mean anything has lost its bite.'

This was Richard Rumelt in his 2011 best seller, *Good Strategy, Bad Strategy*.

He sees bad strategy as expressed often in an interminable PowerPoint presentation, replete with vision, mission, goals and objectives, forcefully expressed and communicated with gusto and apparent conviction. But it is built on sand. It is a propaganda tool, for both staff and investors. Its goals have no bearing on achievable reality.

Bad strategy tends to display one of four hallmarks:

- **Fluff** – esoteric jargon serving to befuddle the reader or listener and convey a sense of 'I know best' to the presenter
- **Waywardness** – insufficient definition of the challenge, therefore no means of properly evaluating the strategy
- **Desire** – goals that are exhortations rather than plans for overcoming challenges
- **Woolliness** – objectives that fail to address critical issues ('dog's dinner') or are impractical ('blue sky').

Good strategy is about the exploitation of two natural sources of strength:

- **Coherence** – creating power through the coherence of a firm design; coordinating policies, resources and action to that end
- **Discovery** – creating new sources of power, often by taking a different perspective on the challenge ahead; thus David's power came from a formidably accurate slingshot to the one weak spot in the armour of the giant Goliath – the forehead.

Good strategy is rooted in **diagnosis** – a thorough analysis of the business challenge ahead, warts and all, the designing of a **guiding policy** ('an approach to dealing with the obstacles called out in the diagnosis'), which will create and sustain a competitive advantage and the translation of that policy into specific and coherent **actions**.

Those three aspects (see Figure 23.1) represent the 'kernel' of a good strategy.

Beyond that, a good strategy works by 'harnessing power' and applying it to where it will have the greatest effect. Rumelt elaborates on nine such power sources, admittedly non-exhaustive but fundamental:

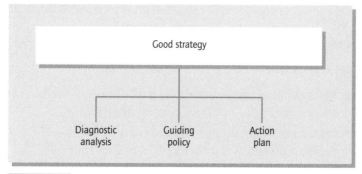

Figure 23.1 **Good strategy**   Source: Adapted from Richard P. Rumelt, *Good Strategy, Bad Strategy: The Difference and Why It Matters*, Profile, 2011

- **Using leverage** – a channelling of activity and energy on a pivotal objective to achieve a tipping point and a 'cascade of favourable outcomes'
- **Proximate objectives** – challenging but attainable objectives (for example the SMART objectives of Tool 3)
- **Chain-link systems** – if there is one link in your chain that is so weak that its breaking will bring down the whole venture, there is no point in strengthening other links until that link is fixed – for example the O-ring in the booster engine of the spacecraft *Challenger* in 1986
- **Using design** – framing the user experience so intimately that it drives product development, engineering, manufacturing and sales
- **Focus** – identify your competitive advantage, don't be swayed into deviation into superficially attractive areas where your advantage counts for little
- **Growth** – this should be the reward for competitive advantage, innovation or efficiency, not for financial engineering through grandiose and value-destroying mergers and acquisitions (see Tool 17)
- **Using advantage** – deepen it, broaden it, reinforce it
- **Using dynamics** – ride the crest of any exogenous new wave, whether technological, environmental or socio-cultural

▪ **Inertia and entropy** – exploit any such organisational shortcomings in your rivals, to which market leaders are particularly prone, and renew your own organisation if and when necessary to repel any such encroachment.

How to use it

By following the 25 need-to-know tools in this book you will avoid many of the pitfalls of bad strategy. Your strategy will have been grounded in Rumelt's diagnosis – the micro-economic analysis of Tools 5 and 6 and the micro-competitive analysis of Tools 7–12, before being rounded off by the risk analysis of Tool 25.

Rumelt's is an immensely readable book, choc-a-bloc with lively, often quirky examples. It opens with Admiral Nelson plotting the destruction of the Spanish fleet at Trafalgar by aiming his more flexible (and outnumbered) ships directly at his foe.

Other strategy exemplars, good, bad or ugly, include General Schwarzkopf, David and Goliath, Iraqi insurgents, NASA's Challenger, Hannibal and Galileo, as well as the more customary likes of Apple, IBM, BMW, GM et al.

When to use it – or be wary

Use Rumelt's book to help you think strategically; read it at leisure and enjoy.

The book contains an element of self-back-slapping, with some examples chosen where the good professor himself has advised wisely. There are also so many examples that it can be difficult at times to see what point is being made and where it fits into the overall scheme of things.

But such shortcomings are par for the genre. Read on and discover the next, surprising and revelatory strategic vignette.

Using it: Wal-Mart

Rumelt likes to use the example of Wal-Mart in his lectures – not the global giant of today, but the start-up of the 1960s.

He invites MBA students to brainstorm the secrets of Sam Walton's success and they come up with a diverse array of answers, like:

- Walton put large stores in small towns
- He kept overheads to a minimum
- He employed non-union labour
- He priced lower than the competition
- He ran a computerised warehousing system.

These are all correct, but miss the essence of Walton's strategy

- Coherence – he created power through his wholly integrated supply chain
- Discovery – he created new sources of power through innovative information systems and logistics.

In essence, he redefined the concept of a 'grocery store'. The former market-leading supermarket chain, Kmart, had a traditional, decentralised structure, where the store manager was the king, making key decisions on what to stock, when and how much to order, and what price to sell them at.

Walton's stores were just outlets. All decisions were made centrally, based on precise information gleaned at the point of sale as to what was selling, how much of it and when the store's supplies would need topping up. The stores were mere nodes in an integrated network.

Thus, as the students surmised, his stores could operate as successfully in a small town as a large town. Thus his store overheads were kept to a minimum. Thus he undercut the competition.

Kmart had to file for Chapter 11 protection from bankruptcy in 2002. Its back was against the Wal.

Innovation hot spots (Gratton)

This tool will help you:

- Understand the importance of creating 'hot spots' in your organisation
- Learn the four main ways of nurturing them – collegiality, inter-departmental collaboration, vision and communication/teamwork
- Ignite your firm

About this tool

Does your organisation have a creative buzz? Should it?

Do your competitors have the buzz? Shouldn't you?

As Linda Gratton asks in her 2007 book, *Innovation Hot Spots: Why Some Companies Buzz with Energy and Innovation... and Others Don't*, why do some companies buzz with energy, innovation and creativity? Why do these flares of activity occur in some companies and teams and not in others? How can you avoid the Big Freeze and instead encourage the creation of these centres of creativity, action and energy?

Gratton says that you always know when you are in a hot spot. You feel energised and vibrantly alive. The atmosphere is charged with a buzz of ideas and dynamic creativity. Hot spots are the 'times and places in some companies and teams where unexpected cooperation and collaboration flourish, creating great energy, productivity and excitement'.

Gratton asked these questions of 57 different companies, from Adidas to Unilever, BP to Goldman Sachs, exploring the conditions and environments that are conducive to the creation of hot spots. She found four essential elements for the nourishing of hot spots:

- **A cooperative mindset** – fostered through a culture of mutuality and collegiality

- **An ability to span boundaries** – working with people with new ideas from outside your group

- **The collective igniting of purpose** – through a vision, challenge or task, to focus energy and not let it dissipate

- **The achieving of productive capacity** – requiring skills of discourse, conflict-resolution and teamwork.

She expressed this as the formula shown in Figure 24.1 to show that each of the first three elements has a multiplicative effect on the others and the absence of one will have a major impact on the potential energy of a hot spot. The capacity of this potential energy to be translated into productive energy – hence innovation and value creation – depends on the productive capacity of the people in the emerging hot spot.

Gratton sees the role of the leader in nurturing hot spots as less one of direction and control but more as orchestrator, process-builder and network creator.

How to use it

Is your firm as innovative as the competition? Should it be? How can you create more buzz, become more innovative? Follow Gratton's approach.

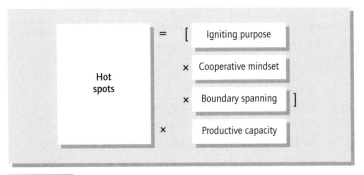

Figure 24.1 Innovation hot spots

Source: Adapted from Linda Gratton, *Innovation Hot Spots:
Why Some Companies Buzz with Energy and Innovation... and Others Don't*, FT Prentice Hall, 2007

When to use it – or be wary

Use this approach when you need to make your firm more innovative.

But it won't happen overnight. The approach may represent a cultural shift for your firm. Tread lightly but steadily.

case study

Using it: Linux

Gratton speaks wondrously of Linux. Created by Finn Linus Torvalds in the early 1990s, building on the work of open-source software pioneers such as Richard Stallman, the operating system has developed over time to become a credible alternative to those of Microsoft and Sun Microsystems.

Unlike the last two, Linux is open source – meaning than the licensor is given the data and opportunity to develop the software further to whatever end, and then release that development back into the community.

The Linux community is largely voluntary. Thousands of software engineers, enthusiasts all, often employed by an international giant, give of their free time to drive the project forward. And with success.

▶ Many large companies and governments are now using Linux, not just for the cost savings but, to some, for the perceived extra flexibility.

Linux is the quintessential hot spot:

- **A cooperative mindset** – they are all like-minded software engineers, somewhat altruistic and, in some ways, the geek equivalent of the commune culture of the 1960s

- **An ability to span boundaries** – almost wholly virtual, so truly global

- **The collective igniting of purpose** – all engaged in the intellectual challenge of getting one step ahead of Microsoft

- **The achieving of productive capacity** – regular sharing of ideas and progress within this online community, along with constructive peer review.

The challenge is how to create a Linux-type environment within your organisation. Gratton says that one such way is to frame a seemingly unsolvable problem that only a fully engaged and genuinely excited set of people can hope to resolve.

Get them feeling 'hot, hot, hot', as Montserrat's Arrow might exhort.

The Suns & Clouds Chart (Evans)

This tool will help you:

- Appreciate that 'in these matters, the only certainty is that nothing is certain' (Pliny the Elder, the Roman military strategist-cum-philosopher)
- Assess the balance of risks and opportunities in your strategy from the dual perspectives of likelihood and impact
- Amend your strategy as appropriate to ensure that the resultant opportunities surpass the risks involved

About this tool

'When written in Chinese the word crisis is composed of two characters. One represents danger, and the other opportunity,' said John F. Kennedy.

Risk and opportunity may indeed be two sides of the same coin. Both are displayed in the Suns & Clouds Chart.

I first created the chart in the early 1990s. Since then I've seen it reproduced in various forms in reports by my consulting competitors. They say imitation is the sincerest form of flattery, but I still kick myself that I didn't copyright it back then!

The reason it keeps getting pinched is that it works. It manages to encapsulate, in one chart, conclusions on the relative importance of all the main strategic issues facing your firm. It shows, diagrammatically and visually, whether the opportunities surpass the risks. Or vice-versa.

In short, in one chart, it tells you whether your strategy is viable. Or not.

How to use it

Assemble all the major risks and opportunities you have identified during your strategy development process. They will include:

- **Market demand risks** – arising, perhaps, from the analysis of Tool 5
- **Industry competition risks** – from Tool 6
- **Competitive position risks** – from Tool 7
- **Business plan risks** – from the implementation of your strategy.

Don't list every risk, or you'll end up with dozens. Focus on the ones that matter – those that will have a big impact if they happen – or those that are likely to happen.

Likewise for opportunities. Try to end up with 6–10 risks and the same number of opportunities.

You are now ready to slot them into a Suns & Clouds Chart.

The chart forces you to view each risk (and opportunity) from two perspectives: how likely it is to happen, and how big an impact it would have if it did (see Figure 25.1). You don't need to quantify the impact, but instead have some idea of the notional, relative impact of each issue on the value of the firm.

In the chart, risks are represented as clouds, opportunities as suns. For each risk (and opportunity), you need to place it in the appropriate position on the chart, taking into account both its likelihood and impact.

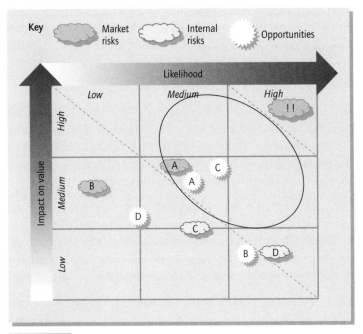

Figure 25.1 The Suns & Clouds Chart

The Suns & Clouds Chart tells you two main things about how viable your strategy is: whether there are any extraordinary risks (or opportunities), and whether the overall balance of risk and opportunity is favourable.

Extraordinary risk

Take a look at the top right-hand corner of the chart. There's a heavy thundercloud in there, with two exclamation marks. That's a risk that is both very likely and very big. It's a showstopper risk. If you find one of them, your strategy is unviable.

The closer a cloud gets to that thundercloud, the worse news it is. Risks that hover around the diagonal (from the top-left to the bottom-right corners) can be handled, as long as they are balanced by opportunities. But, as soon as a cloud starts creeping towards that thundercloud, for example to around where opportunity B is placed, that's when you should start to worry.

But imagine a bright shining sun in that spot where the thunder-cloud is. That's terrific news, and you'll have suitors clambering over each other to back you.

The balance

In general there's no showstopper risk. The main purpose of the Suns & Clouds Chart then will be to present the **balance** of risk and opportunity. Do the opportunities surpass the risks? Given the overall picture, are the suns more favourably placed than the clouds? Or do the clouds overshadow the suns?

The way to assess a Suns & Clouds Chart is to look first at the general area above the diagonal and in the direction of the thun-dercloud. This is the area covered in Figure 25.1 by the parabola. Any risk (or opportunity) there is worthy of note: it's at least rea-sonably likely to occur **and** would have at least a reasonable impact.

Those risks and opportunities below the diagonal are less important. They are either of low-to-medium likelihood **and** of low-to-medium impact, or they're not big enough, or not likely enough, to be of major concern.

Take a look at the pattern of suns and clouds in your chart around the area of the parabola. The closer each sun and cloud is to the thundercloud, the more important it is. If the pattern of suns seems better placed than the pattern of clouds, your strategy may be sound.

In the chart above, there are two clouds and two suns above the diagonal. But risk D lies outside the parabola. The best placed is opportunity B. Risk A and opportunity A more or less bal-ance each other out, likewise other risks and opportunities. Opportunity B seems distinctly clear of the pack. The opportuni-ties seem to surpass the risks. The business looks viable.

One of the best features of the Suns & Clouds Chart is that it can be made dynamic. If the balance of risk and opportunity shown on the chart is unfavourable, you may be able to do something about it – and the chart will show this clearly.

For every risk, there are mitigating factors. Many, including those relating to market demand and competition (the darker clouds in Figure 25.1), will be beyond your control. Those relating to your firm's competitive position, however, are within your power to influence. They may, indeed, be an integral part of your emergent strategy.

Likewise, your strategy may improve the likelihood of achieving a key opportunity on the chart, thereby shifting the sun to the right.

Risk mitigation or opportunity enhancement in the Suns & Clouds Chart can be illuminated with arrows and target signs. They'll show where your firm should aim for and remind you that it's a target. It should improve the overall balance of risk and opportunity in your strategy.

When to use it – or be wary

You can use the Suns & Clouds Chart in so many situations. It was designed for purposes of strategic due diligence in transactions such as acquisitions, alliances and investments, but it is just as useful in project appraisal, strategy review (as here) or even in career development and change – see my book *Backing U!: A Business-Oriented Guide to Backing Your Passion and Achieving Career Success*. It could even be useful in spotting emergent talent in the world of entertainment (see 'Using it: Madonna').

Don't worry if your Suns & Clouds Chart doesn't make that much sense initially. This chart changes with further thought and discussion. **Always.** Arguably its greatest virtue is its stimulus to discussion. It provokes amendment.

Remember, you cannot be exact in this chart. Nor do you need to be. It is a pictorial representation of risk and opportunity, designed to give you a **feel** for the balance of risk and opportunity in your strategy.

What about highly improbable but potentially catastrophic risks, you might ask? The chart deals with them, too. In the autumn of 2001, my colleagues and I were advising a client on whether to back a company involved in airport operations. After the first week of work, we produced an interim report and a first-cut Suns & Clouds Chart. In the top left-hand corner box, we placed a risk entitled 'major air incident'. We were thinking of a serious air crash that might lead to the prolonged grounding of a common class of aircraft. It seemed unlikely, but would have a very large impact if it happened.

9/11 came just a few days later. We never envisaged anything so devastating, so inconceivably evil, but at least we had alerted our client to the extreme risks involved in the air industry. The deal was renegotiated and completed successfully.

---

case study

Using it: Madonna

Suppose you're an investor. It's 1982 and you show up at a grubby studio in downtown Manhattan to meet a young woman with grandiose aspirations of stardom. Ms Ciccone is a dancer who can sing a bit. She's a hard worker, but she's hard up. She's been scraping a living in New York City for five years, through a succession of low-paid jobs, including nude modelling.

She has made some progress as an entertainer. She has worked with a number of modern dance companies, been a backing dancer on a world tour and played vocals and drums with a rock band, the Breakfast Club. She has written and produced a number of solo disco and dance songs – and has signed a singles deal with Sire Records. Her first single, *Everybody*, written by herself and for which she received $5,000, is proving quite a hit on the dance charts and in the clubs. However, it has made no impact on the Billboard Hot 100.

Would you have backed her? On the basis of the Suns & Clouds Chart alone, possibly not – see Figure 25.2. Music trends were moving in other directions. *Everybody* was successful only in the small niche of club music. She might have followed that up with another single or two, even an album. But they, too, might have found just a niche following. She was, basically, a dancer, with a rather screechy voice. She dressed and looked sexy, but so did loads of other dancers.

Risks

1. Dance scene led by black bands (e.g., Kool, Michael Jackson)
2. Moving to new pop (e.g., Human League, Men At Work)
3. Female artists more into soul (e.g., Diana Ross) or ballad (e.g., Olivia N-J) than rock (e.g., Tina Turner)
4. Madonna's high-energy dance music pitch too narrow a market
5. Madonna has limited singing talent

Opportunities

1. *Everybody* had niche club following, so too for follow-up singles?
2. Likewise with a first album
3. Madonna seems highly driven and committed to self-promotion
4. She could be packaged for new pop video market of MTV
5. Madonna could create new genre of white, female, dance rock?

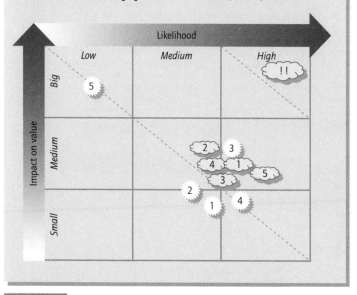

Figure 25.2 Would you have backed Madonna in 1982?

But you may have seen something else. One opportunity (sun 3) may have stood out. You would have spent some time with her and caught a glimpse of what many later came to recognise: a relentless drive, evidenced by her painstaking build-up of performing experience in those early years; a steely professionalism; an extroversion bordering on the exhibitionist, with a readiness to blend her very person with her image; boundless ambition. This was special. You may well have backed her.

One year later and her Suns & Clouds Chart (Figure 25.3) would have changed beyond recognition. Her first album, *Madonna*, reached the top 10 in the album charts and 5 of its singles became hits. One of them, *Holiday*, went on to sell 12 million copies. The main risks concerning the breadth of her appeal would have evaporated. The main opportunity – of her being able to carve out a new genre of white, female dance-rock music with huge popular appeal – was now looking not just conceivable but likely.

Risks

Opportunities

1. Dance scene led by black bands (e.g., Kool, Michael Jackson)
2. Moving to new pop (e.g., Human League, Men At Work)
3. Female artists more into soul (e.g., Diana Ross) or ballad (e.g., Olivia N-J) than rock (e.g., Tina Turner)
4. Madonna's high-energy dance music pitch too narrow a market
5. Madonna has limited singing talent

1. *Everybody* had niche club following, so too for follow-up singles?
2. Likewise with a first album
3. Madonna seems highly driven and committed to self-promotion
4. She could be packaged for new pop video market of MTV
5. Madonna could create new genre of white, female, dance rock?

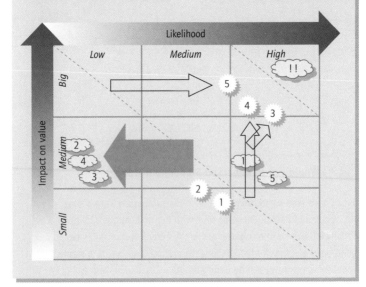

Figure 25.3 Would you have backed Madonna one year later?!

If you hadn't backed her the year before, you wouldn't be able to afford to now. Opportunities were unbounded.

Fast forward now to 1992. In the interim, albums such as *Like a Virgin, True Blue,* and *Like a Prayer* had kept Madonna at the top of the charts. She had even received critical acclaim in a movie, *Desperately Seeking Susan.*

Then along came *Sex,* a coffee-table book of photographs featuring Madonna in an array of sexually explicit poses. It was damned by the media as narcissistic, some said pornographic. *Erotica* soon followed, an album that met with similar disdain. The video accompanying the (successful) lead single was withdrawn from MTV. Then Madonna took the leading female role in a movie, *Body of Evidence*, a smuttier take on *Basic Instinct.* It flopped.

Had Madonna blown it? Had her star waned? Were these ventures into sexual explicitness just a sad, final fling for an entertainer who had passed her sell-by date?

Would you have backed her then? Could she ever recover from such a critical mauling, from an apparent obliteration of her fan base? Could she ever generate again the kind of multimillion-dollar income stream she had achieved in the 1980s?

You may well have done. For all the risks, the dominant feature in Madonna's latest Suns & Clouds Chart would have been her consistent strategy. If that had to be encapsulated in one sentence, which is what a good strategy should be, it could have been: 'To build on her capabilities in the performing arts through sustained investment of cash, time and energy in image reinvention and self-publicity.'

That strategy may have dragged down her fortunes in 1992, but surely it could, just as easily, yank them up again in years to come? And, perhaps, she may have learned some lessons from the debacle and be a trifle more circumspect in her future reinventions? Her chart may have looked like Figure 25.4.

The one thing you know for sure in the world of entertainment is that performers must keep their name in the headlines, their face on the front covers of magazines, whether in praise or condemnation. Any news is good news. No news is obscurity. In her year of sexual exhibitionism, Madonna had been very much the news. All she had to do next was reinvent herself again, preferably into something less controversial – an Argentinean folk heroine, perhaps, or an Eastern mystic, or an all-American girl, or a devoted mother, or a lady of the manor, whatever – and she could postpone her sell-by date indefinitely.

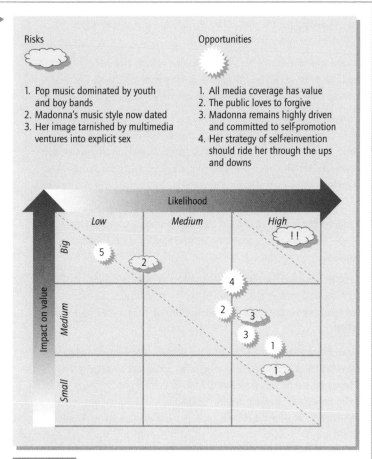

Risks

1. Pop music dominated by youth and boy bands
2. Madonna's music style now dated
3. Her image tarnished by multimedia ventures into explicit sex

Opportunities

1. All media coverage has value
2. The public loves to forgive
3. Madonna remains highly driven and committed to self-promotion
4. Her strategy of self-reinvention should ride her through the ups and downs

Figure 25.4 Would you have backed Madonna ten years later?

The strategy was brilliant. Surely you would have backed her. She would go on to achieve the highest grossing concert tour by a female artist ever, the controversial *Confessions* tour. Later she would break that record again with her *MDNA* and *Sticky & Sweet* tours.

A material girl indeed.

Conclusion

A final cautionary word from Michael Porter: 'The company without a strategy is willing to try anything.'

Yours won't be one such company. By applying the 25 tools of this book, you should be well on the way towards developing a robust strategy for your firm.

There are, of course, many, many more strategy tools, perhaps not as essential as those set out in this book, but nevertheless useful for specific tasks and in certain circumstances.

Tools such as Stern Stewart's Economic Value Added, Kano's product quality and satisfaction and Collis and Montgomery's Strategically Valuable Resources may be pertinent to your firm in your situation.

Other, more generic, tools such as scenario planning, making the strategic investment decision and using expected value and sensitivity analysis may also be useful to you.

All these and many more are to be found in this book's elder sister: *Key Strategy Tools: The 80+ Tools for Every Manager to Build a Winning Strategy.*

Or you may need further guidance not just in specific tools but in the strategy development process itself. That can be found in my book *The FT Essential Guide to Developing a Business Strategy: How to Use Strategic Planning to Start Up or Grow Your Business,* which takes you through the whole process via a central case study running throughout as well as a number of real-life case studies.

But the 25 tools of this book are, arguably, the most important that you'll need for drawing up a strategy – and that is why they were selected.

Enjoy and best of luck!

What did you think of this book?

We're really keen to hear from you about this book, so that we can make our publishing even better.

Please log on to the following website and leave us your feedback.

It will only take a few minutes and your thoughts are invaluable to us.

www.pearsoned.co.uk/bookfeedback

Ten useful strategy books to read next

Here are 10 books that I would recommend for every strategist wanting to find out more:

1   Christensen, Clayton M. (1997) *The Innovator's Dilemma: When New Technologies Cause Great Firms to Fail*, Harvard Business School Press.

    How to do everything right yet still crash, an earth-shattering book upon launch.

2   Collins, James C. and Porras, Jerry I. (1997) *Built to Last: Successful Habits of Visionary Companies*, Random House.

    Why vision and big, hairy, audacious goals drive sustained success.

3   Evans, Vaughan (2013) *The FT Essential Guide to Developing a Business Strategy: How to Use Strategic Planning to Start Up or Grow Your Business*, FT Publishing.

    Save yourself mega-bucks in consulting fees with this succinct, practical and lively DIY guide.

4   Goddard, Jules and Eccles, Tony (2013) *Uncommon Sense, Common Nonsense: Why Some Organisations Consistently Outperform Others*, Profile Books.

    Provocative: what did BMW spot in the Mini that previous owners hadn't?

5 Grant, Robert M. (2013) *Contemporary Strategy Analysis*, 8th edition, Wiley-Blackwell.

The one and only strategy textbook, in its third decade.

6 Gratton, Linda (2007) *Innovation Hot Spots: Why Some Companies Buzz with Energy and Innovation... and Others Don't*, FT Prentice Hall.

Purpose, cooperation and border-crossing vision and togetherness are what spark a climate of innovation.

7 Kim, W. Chan and Mauborgne, Renée (2005) *Blue Ocean Strategy: How to Create Uncontested Market Space and Make the Competition Irrelevant*, Harvard Business School Press.

Finally, a contender to Porter's magnum opus (below).

8 Mintzberg, Henry (1994) *The Rise and Fall of Strategic Planning*, Free Press.

Iconoclastic, the 'suck-it-and-see' alternative to strategic planning.

9 Mullins, John (2013) *The New Business Road Test: What Entrepreneurs and Executives Should Do Before Writing a Business Plan*, 4th edition, FT Prentice Hall.

Strategy made real for business start-ups.

10 Porter, Michael E. (1984) *Competitive Advantage*, Free Press.

The bible of strategy, peerless since the early 1980s.

Glossary of terms

Advantage See **competitive advantage**.

Attractiveness See **market attractiveness**.

Blue oceans Uncontested market space, as distinct from the 'red oceans' of existing market space (Tool 15).

Business Strategic business unit.

Business strategy Gaining a sustainable competitive advantage in a single strategic business unit.

Capabilities How a firm deploys its resources.

Capability gap The gap in performance between where your firm is currently positioned against key success factors and where it aims to be.

Competitive advantage The strategic advantage possessed by one firm over others in a product/market segment or industry, which enables it to make superior returns.

Competitive intensity The degree of competition in a given industry and a main determinant of industry profitability (Tool 6).

Competitive position A rating of a firm's relative competitiveness in a given product/market segment or industry (Tool 7).

Complement The opposite of a substitute – where an increase in demand for one good (or service) results in an increase in demand for another.

Core competence An integrated bundle of skills and technologies; the sum of learning across individual skill sets and individual organisational units (Tool 19).

Corporate strategy Optimising value from a portfolio of businesses and adding value to each through exploiting the firm's core resources and capabilities.

Customer purchasing criteria (CPCs) What customers need from their suppliers (Tool 7).

Disruptive technology One that radically alters the benefit/price algorithm (Tool 22).

Diversification Moving away from your core business (Tool 10).

Economies of scale The reduction in unit costs in a firm arising from an increase in the scale of its operations.

Economies of scope The reduction in unit costs in a firm arising from the production of similar or related goods or services.

Emergent strategy That which emerges over time as intentions collide with and respond to a changing reality (Tool 20).

Experience curve An effect whereby the unit cost of a standard product declines by a constant percentage each time cumulative output doubles (Tool 14).

Five forces Key forces driving industry competition, namely internal rivalry, new entrants, substitutes, supplier bargaining power and customer bargaining power (Tool 6).

Generic strategies Those that relate to an entire genus or class, namely differentiation, low-cost or focus strategies (Tool 13).

'HOOF approach Forecasting market demand by assessing the historic (H) rate of growth, identifying key drivers (D), assessing how these and potentially new drivers may change in the future (D) and thereby deriving demand forecasts (F) (Tool 5).

Ideal player The theoretical competitor who achieves the highest possible rating against each key success factor.

Industry maturity The stage of evolution of an industry, from embryonic through to growing, mature and ageing.

Industry supply The aggregate supply by producers of a product (or product group) over a specified period of time, typically one year.

Innovation hot spots The times and places in some companies and teams where unexpected cooperation and collaboration flourish, creating great energy, productivity and excitement (Tool 24).

Innovator's dilemma Do you or do you not invest heavily, with inevitable cannibalisation of existing sales, to protect against the possibility of an upstart doing likewise (Tool 22)?

Issue A matter under discussion or in dispute, often due to future uncertainty – a risk or an opportunity.

Key success factors (KSFs) What firms need to do to meet customer purchasing criteria and run a sound business (Tool 7).

Macro-economics The study of the aggregate economy, whether regional, national or international.

Market attractiveness A composite measure of the relative attractiveness of a product/market segment, taking into account factors such as market size, market growth, competitive intensity, industry profitability and market risk (Tool 11).

Marketcrafting Creating estimates of market size (and growth) and market share (and growth) from the bottom up, by using index numbers to gauge the relative scale of key producers, present and past (Tool 5).

Market demand The aggregate demands of customers for a product (or product group) over a specified period of time, typically one year (Tool 5).

Market-positioning school Proponents of the view that strategy should be focused at the level of the business, where all meaningful competition resides, and corporate strategy limited to portfolio planning.

Micro-economics The study of small economic units, such as the consumer, the household, the non-profit organisation or, most commonly, the firm.

Moving average A method of smoothing a time series (typically annual) by averaging a fixed number of consecutive terms (typically three years).

Parenting advantage The creation of synergies not just between strategic business units but between them and the centre (Tool 18).

Portfolio The collection of key product/market segments in a business or of businesses (strategic business units) in a multi-business company.

Price elasticity of demand The percentage change in demand for a good (or service) divided by the percentage change in price.

Profit from the core Build power in a well-defined core (Tool 21).

Relative market share (RMS) Your market share relative to that of your largest competitor (Tool 12).

Resource-based school Proponents of the view that strategy should be focused on leveraging the resources and capabilities of the corporation as a whole (Tools 8 and 19).

Resources A firm's productive assets, whether human, physical, financial or intangible, as distinct from capabilities, which are how a firm deploys its resources.

SBU See **strategic business unit**.

Scenario A coherent and consistent portrayal of a series of future events based on specific parameter assumptions made by the strategist.

Segment A slice of business where the firm sells one product (or product group) to one customer group (strictly a 'product/market segment', Tool 1).

Sensitivity analysis The tweaking of parameter value assumptions to test overall impact on key financials.

Shareholder value The value a shareholder gains from investing in a firm through dividend and other payouts and capital appreciation/gain upon exit.

SMART objectives Those that are specific, measurable, attainable, relevant and time-limited (Tool 3).

SME Small to medium-sized enterprise.

Stakeholder Persons and organisations with a non-shareholding stake in the success of the firm, for example employees, customers, suppliers, national and local government, the local community.

Strategic business unit (SBU) A profit centre entity with a closely inter-related product (or service) offering and a cost structure largely independent of other business units.

Strategic due diligence (aka **market or commercial due diligence**) An assessment of the key risks and opportunities in market demand, industry competition, competitive position, strategy and the business plan facing a target company (Tool 25).

Strategic investment decision Go/no-go decision on an investment of strategic importance.

Strategic resources Those that are valuable, rare, inimitable and non-substitutable (Tool 8).

Strategic repositioning Adjusting strategic position through investing, holding, exiting or entering segments (for business strategy) or businesses (for corporate strategy).

Strategy How a firm achieves its goals by deploying its scarce resources to gain a sustainable competitive advantage.

Structured interviewing Systematised interviewing of customers, suppliers and other industry observers to gain strategic information.

Substitute The opposite of a complement – where an increase in demand for one good or service results in a decrease in demand for another.

Suns & Clouds Chart An assessment of key risks and opportunities, portrayed visually as suns and clouds, by likelihood of occurrence and value impact, should they occur (Tool 25).

Synergy Where the whole is greater than the sum of the parts and, specifically in mergers, acquisitions and alliances, where the value of the merged entity is greater than the pre-bid stand-alone value of the acquirer plus that of the target/partner (Tool 17).

Value chain The key primary and support activities of a firm (Tool 9).

White space The large, but mostly unoccupied, territory in a company where rules are vague, strategy is unclear and where entrepreneurial activity most often takes place (Tool 20).

References and further reading

Tool 1

Bridges, William (1998) *Creating You & Co: Learn to Think Like the CEO of Your Own Career*, Da Capo Press.

Evans, Vaughan (2011) *The FT Essential Guide to Writing a Business Plan: How to Win Backing to Start Up or Grow Your Business*, FT Publishing.

Mullins, John (2013) *The New Business Road Test: What Entrepreneurs and Executives Should Do Before Writing a Business Pla*n, 4th edition, FT Publishing.

Tool 2

Latham, Gary P. and Locke, Edwin A. 'Building a Practically Useful Theory of Goal Setting and Task Motivation', *American Psychologist*, September 2002.

Tool 3

Doran, G.T. 'There's a S.M.A.R.T. Way to Write Management's Goals and Objectives', *Management Review*, November 1981.

Tool 4

Collins, James C. and Porras, Jerry I. (1997) *Built to Last: Successful Habits of Visionary Companies*, Random House.

Tool 5

Evans, Vaughan (2013) *The FT Essential Guide to Developing a Business Strategy: How to Use Strategic Planning to Start Up or Grow Your Business*, FT Publishing.

Tool 6

Porter, Michael E. (1980) *Competitive Strategy: Techniques for Analyzing Industries and Competitors*, Free Press.

Tool 7

Evans, Vaughan (2012) *Key Strategy Tools: The 80+ Tools for Every Manager to Build a Winning Strategy*, FT Publishing.

Tool 8

Grant, Robert M. (2013) *Contemporary Strategy Analysis*, 8th edition, Blackwell.

Tool 9

Porter, Michael E. (1980) *Competitive Strategy: Techniques for Analyzing Industries and Competitors*, Free Press.

Tool 10

Ansoff, Igor M. (1965) *Corporate Strategy*, McGraw Hill.

Tool 11

Evans, Vaughan (2013) *The FT Essential Guide to Developing a Business Strategy: How to Use Strategic Planning to Start Up or Grow Your Business*, FT Publishing.

Tool 12

The Boston Consulting Group (www.bcg.com) on *The Growth/Share Matrix*.

Tool 13

Goddard, Jules (2013) 'The Fatal Bias', Chartered Management Institute's Management Article of the Year.

Goddard, Jules and Eccles, Tony (2012) *Uncommon Sense, Common Nonsense: Why Some Organisations Consistently Outperform Others*, Profile.

Porter, Michael E. (1980) *Competitive Strategy: Techniques for Analyzing Industries and Competitors*, Free Press.

Tool 14

Henderson, Bruce (1973) *The Experience Curve Reviewed*, (reprint No. 135), The Boston Consulting Group.

Lund University (2006) *New Energy Externalities Developments for Sustainability: Cost Development – an Analysis Based on Experience Curves*.

Tool 15

Kim, W. Chan and Mauborgne, Renée (2005) *Blue Ocean Strategy: How to Create Uncontested Market Space and Make the Competition Irrelevant*, Harvard Business School Press.

Tool 16

Drucker, Peter F. (1954) *The Practice of Management*, HarperCollins.

Tool 17

Evans, Vaughan (2012) *Key Strategy Tools: The 80+ Tools for Every Manager to Build a Winning Strategy*, FT Publishing.

Tool 18

Goold, Michael, Campbell, Andrew and Alexander, Marcus (1994) *Corporate-Level Strategy: Creating Value in the Multi-Business Company*, Wiley.

Tool 19

Hamel, Gary and Prahalad, C.K. (1994) *Competing for the Future*, Harvard Business School Press.

Tool 20

Hartung, Adam 'How Facebook Beat MySpace', *Forbes.com*, 14 January 2011.

Maletz, Mark C. and Nohria, Nitin 'Managing in the Whitespace', *Harvard Business Review*, February 2001.

Mintzberg, Henry (1994) *The Rise and Fall of Strategic Planning*, Free Press.

Tool 21

Peters, Tom and Waterman Jr, Robert H. (1982) *In Search of Excellence: Lessons from America's Best Run Companies*, Profile.

Zook, Chris (2001) *Profit from the Core*, Harvard Business Press.

Tool 22

Christensen, Clayton M. (1997) *The Innovator's Dilemma: When New Technologies Cause Great Firms to Fail*, Harvard Business School Press.

Tool 23

Rumelt, Richard P. (2011) *Good Strategy, Bad Strategy: The Difference and Why It Matters*, Profile.

Tool 24

Gratton, Linda (2007) *Innovation Hot Spots: Why Some Companies Buzz with Energy and Innovation... and Others Don't*, FT Prentice Hall.

Tool 25

Evans, Vaughan (2009) *Backing U!: A Business-Oriented Guide to Backing Your Passion and Achieving Career Success*, Business and Careers Press.

Index

Page numbers in *italics* refer to a figure/table
Page numbers in **bold** refer to glossary definitions

Do you want your people to be the very best at what they do?

Talk to us about how we can help.

As the world's leading learning company, we know a lot about what your people need in order to be better at what they do.

Whatever subject or skills you've got in mind (from presenting or persuasion to coaching or communication skills), and at whatever level (from new-starters through to top executives) we can help you deliver tried-and-tested, essential learning straight to your workforce – whatever they need, whenever they need it and wherever they are.

Talk to us today about how we can:

- Complement and support your existing learning and development programmes
- Enhance and augment your people's learning experience
- Match your needs to the best of our content
- Customise, brand and change it to make a better fit
- Deliver cost-effective, great value learning content that's proven to work.

Contact us today:
corporate.enquiries@pearson.com

ALWAYS LEARNING

PEARSON